Beginning
MICROWAVE
COOKERY

Beginning MICROWAVE COOKERY

Margaret Weale

ANGELL EDITIONS

Newton Abbot, Devon

Acknowledgements

William Adams (member of the Wedgwood Group)
Birds Eye Wall's Ltd

Photography: Stan Weale
Design: Michael Head
Typesetting: Ace Filmsetting, Frome
Colour separations: Gilchrist Brothers, Leeds
Printing and binding: Royal Smeets Offset b.v., Weert

Printed in the Netherlands for
Angell Editions Limited
39 Coombeshead Road
Newton Abbot, Devon

British Library Cataloguing in Publication Data
Weale, Margaret
  Beginning microwave cookery.
  1. Microwave cookery
  I. Title
  641.5'882   TX832

Hardback ISBN 0 948432 10 1
Paperback ISBN 0 948432 05 5

Contents

Introduction

You are probably one of the many new proud owners of a microwave oven and, having read the manufacturer's instructions, are now eager to start cooking. Like all appliances, a microwave oven does have certain limitations which must be recognised. You will still need a conventional cooker for making toast, pancakes, hard boiling eggs in their shells and deep-fat frying. A conventional oven will still be used for roast potatoes, Yorkshire pudding, many pastry dishes, baked soufflés and other foods that require a dry heat to retain their shape or to crisp and brown them. However, used in conjunction with your conventional cooking appliances and home freezer, a microwave oven will enable you to cook a wide variety of foods in the minimum amount of time with fewer dishes to wash up at the end of a meal. Providing meals for your family and friends will become an enjoyable experience.

A microwave oven is easy to use, once you know how. Cooking food, by any method, is an art and requires patience to achieve perfect results. Once you have mastered the art of microwave cooking you will, like me, wonder how you ever managed without this exciting domestic appliance. But cooking by microwave energy does differ from cooking conventionally, and there are a few basic techniques which must be observed for successful results.

Basic techniques

Timing

One of the things you will find difficult to appreciate, initially, is the speed of defrosting, reheating and cooking. Correct timing is essential, and the golden rule in microwave cooking is to undercook rather than risk overcooking.

Undercooked food can always be returned to the oven, but there is no remedy for overcooking. To begin with, watch food as it cooks, and check it regularly. Times given throughout this book for defrosting, reheating and cooking food should be used as a guide only, since ovens do vary from one model to another.

Timing will be affected by:

Oven output The higher the oven output, the faster it will cook food and vice versa.

Quantity of food Small quantities of food will cook in less time than larger quantities of the same food. For instance, one jacket potato will require less time to cook than two jacket potatoes. As a guide, when you double the amount of food the cooking time is generally increased by between one third and one half. Similarly, when you halve the amount of food the cooking time should be decreased to slightly more than half the time given for the full quantity.

Starting temperature of food Food taken straight from a refrigerator will take longer to heat and cook than food at room temperature. In the same way, frozen food will take longer to heat and cook than refrigerated food. Kitchen temperatures also vary, depending on the time of year, so you may find if necessary to extend cooking times very slightly on cold wintry days.

Food composition Foods with a high fat or sugar content will heat more quickly than foods low in fat and sugar. For example, the jam in the centre of a jam doughnut will be much hotter than the surrounding dough, and the fat on meat and poultry will heat more quickly than the leaner meat.

Density of food Dense foods such as joints of meat take longer to defrost, reheat or cook than porous foods such as bread, cakes and puddings.

Size and shape of food Microwaves penetrate food to a depth of 3.75cm (1½in), so smaller thinner pieces will cook more quickly than larger thicker pieces of the same food. For even cooking results, it is therefore important to cut meat and vegetables into even-sized pieces. Boned and rolled joints of meat will cook more evenly than irregularly shaped joints. For instance, a leg of lamb should be shielded at the narrow end with a small piece of smooth aluminium foil for about half the cooking time, to prevent it being overcooked before the thicker part of the joint is ready. Foil must never be allowed to touch any part of the oven interior.

Moisture content of food Food with a high moisture content will take longer to cook than less moist food. e.g. vegetables cooked in a small amount of water, as recommended in this book, will cook in less time than if a larger quantity of water is added. Microwaves are attracted to moisture, which is present in all foods.

Size and shape of cooking container Food placed in a larger dish will cook more quickly than the same amount of food heaped up in a smaller deeper dish. The shape of the dish will also affect cooking times.

Raw ingredients The quality and age of raw ingredients will affect not only the cooking time but also the end results. For best results use only good quality raw ingredients.

Personal preference Some of us prefer foods less well done than others. Increase or decrease the cooking times given in this book to suit you and your family.

Arranging food
Always place the thicker parts of food towards the outside of the dish. For example, to cook chicken drumsticks arrange the thick meatier parts towards the outside of the dish and the thinner bone ends towards the centre. Also when cooking more than two jacket potatoes or other individual foods, arrange them in a circle with space between them. Spread food out in an even layer, avoiding mounds, especially in the centre.

Foods with skin or membrane
Foods with skin such as sausages, unpeeled apples, jacket potatoes and whole tomatoes should be pricked to prevent bursting during cooking. For the same reason the membrane covering kidneys and egg yolks should be pricked. Always try to use eggs at room temperature for baked or poached eggs, and never attept to boil eggs in their shells in a microwave oven unless the manufacturer suggests a special way of doing this.

Stirring and turning
When cooking conventionally many foods have to be stirred or turned and the same applies when defrosting, reheating or cooking in a microwave oven. The outer edges of food normally cook first in a microwave oven, so stirring during cooking gives more even results in a shorter time. When food is to be stirred, the outer cooked edges should be brought towards the centre of the dish and the less cooked centre portion moved towards the outside. Other foods such as joints of meat, poultry and jacket potatoes are turned over during cooking so that they cook more evenly. The same techniques apply when defrosting frozen food, to ensure more even thawing. Recipes in this book have been tested mainly in ovens with turntables. If your oven does not have this facility you may find it necessary to rotate dishes, giving them a quarter or half turn during defrosting, reheating and cooking.

Standing time
Food continues to cook after it is removed from a microwave oven, and allowances have been made for this in the defrosting, reheating and cooking times given throughout this book. Initially you may have difficulty in assessing when to remove food from the oven. The golden rule is to remove it sooner rather than later, leave it to stand for the recommended time and only then, if necessary, return it to the oven for further cooking.

To cover or not to cover
Just as when cooking conventionally, some

foods are covered while others are left uncovered. When it is essential to retain steam and moisture, food is covered. Plastic wrap and tight-fitting lids will retain more heat than loose-fitting lids and will ensure faster, more even cooking. Other foods which you wish to keep dry, such as bread and cakes, are not covered. Foods which splatter, such as bacon, are covered loosely with kitchen or greaseproof paper. When food is to be covered, this is stated in the recipe. Otherwise leave uncovered.

Browning
Microwave cooking is a moist form of cooking. It is also very fast, so small items of food such as chicken portions, sausages and chops, and porous items such as bread and cakes, do not brown as when cooked conventionally. Larger joints of meat, large chickens and turkey will brown during their longer cooking times, but their skin will not be crisp. Cooking small joints of meat and small chickens in pierced roasting bags will encourage browning, but again the skin will not be crisp. Many foods can be browned or crisped by placing them under a preheated conventional grill or in a conventional oven at the end of the microwave cooking time. The appearance of meat and poultry can be improved by using the special microwave seasonings and coatings which are now available. Chops, sausages, burgers and crumb-coated foods are best cooked in a special microwave browning dish (page 12). Dark-coloured cakes, such as chocolate cakes,

are obviously acceptable in colour, and light-coloured cakes can be attractively decorated to compensate for their paleness.

Care, cleaning and maintenance
Refer to the detailed information on care, cleaning and maintenance given in the Users' Instructions supplied with your particular model of oven. Remove any marks or spillage from the oven after use, paying particular attention to the door area and door seal. Any food particles left in the oven will absorb microwave energy, slow down cooking, and become more difficult to remove.

Power output levels used in this book
Most microwave ovens now have at least two power output levels. HIGH or FULL POWER setting is used to cook most foods quickly. LOW or DEFROST setting is used not only to defrost frozen foods but also to cook certain foods which benefit from longer slower cooking, such as meat casseroles and baked egg custard. These are the two settings which are used throughout this book and they are based on ovens with a maximum output of approximately 650W–700W on HIGH or FULL POWER, and a lower output of approximately 200W–260W. For ovens with lower outputs than these, times will have to be increased slightly. Times given throughout this book should be used as a guide only, since ovens, even with the same output, vary in efficiency.

Cooking containers and utensils

One of the many advantages of a microwave oven is that many foods can be cooked and served in the same dish, so washing up is reduced to a minimum. There is no need to rush out and buy a completely new range of cooking equipment because you will find that many of the containers and utensils you already have in your kitchen are suitable. You won't be using your metal saucepans or baking tins or anything with a metallic trim or manufacturer's mark in silver or gold on the base, but you will be using some things which you have never used in a conventional oven such as special plastics, absorbent kitchen paper, paper plates and white paper napkins. Do not use coloured paper napkins since the colour may transfer to the food. Suitable containers remain relatively cool during cooking, but since heat is transferred from the hot food to the cooking dish it can get hot, especially when cooking foods with a high fat or sugar content. You may therefore find it necessary to use a cloth or oven gloves to remove the dish from the oven. Foods with a high fat or sugar content can reach high temperatures in a short time, so it is essential to use containers with a wide temperature tolerance.

Size and shape
It is important to select the correct size and shape of container since this will affect the cooking time, the attention required during cooking, and the end result.

The size of the container should match the amount of food, and dishes should only be half to two-thirds full. When cooking foods such as soups, rice, pasta and preserves, it is essential to use large containers to prevent spillage. Food cooked in larger shallow dishes which allow a greater area of food surface to be exposed to microwave energy will cook faster than the same amount of food cooked in a smaller deeper dish. On the other hand if a small quantity of food is cooked in too large a dish, any saucy portions will tend to spread out and overcook around the outside before the centre is cooked.

The shape of the container should be carefully chosen. Straight-sided dishes are preferable to those with sloping sides. Round dishes offer more even heating and cooking than oval dishes. Square dishes should have rounded corners to prevent overcooking in these areas. Rectangular dishes are least successful, and require more attention during the cooking period to obtain evenly cooked results. Non-metallic ring moulds give excellent results, especially when cooking foods which cannot be stirred, e.g. cakes. If you do not have a ring mould, you can improvise by placing a glass tumbler (not lead crystal) or glass jar in the centre of a suitable container.

Testing for suitability
If in doubt as to whether or not a container is suitable for use in a microwave oven, you should carry out this simple test. Place the container in the oven with an inch of water and microwave on HIGH for 1½ min if ceramic or glass, or only 10–15 sec if plastic. If the water is hot and the container is cool, it is suitable for use. If, on the other hand, the water is cool and the container is hot, it is unsuitable. If the water is lukewarm and the container is warm this means that the container is absorbing some microwave energy and, although it could be used, it will be less efficient and cooking times will have to be increased.

Glass
Ovenproof glassware and glass ceramic dishes, without metal trim, perform extremely well in a microwave oven. Clear glass ovenware such as Pyrex measuring jugs, soufflé dishes, bowls, casseroles and plates are ideal. This is especially so for the new owner of a microwave oven, because you can see how food is cooking, and at the end of the cooking period you can, for instance, see if the centre base of a cake or pudding is cooked before turning it out of the container. Table glass, such as tumblers, should be used for short-term heating only. Lead crystal and antique glass should not be used.

China and pottery
Provided they do not have a metal trim or manufacturer's mark in silver or gold on the base, sturdy china and pottery dishes are suitable.

Barbecue-style chicken (page 60); Baked celery cheese (page 77); Parsleyed new potatoes (page 70)

Earthenware should have a glazed surface, otherwise it will absorb moisture, deprive the food of microwave energy, extend cooking times, and get very hot. Some pottery is less efficient than others, and can slow down the cooking process. Do not use cups which have had their handles glued on, otherwise the glue will melt.

Paper utensils

Paper cups, plates, napkins and kitchen towels can all be used for short-term heating and cooking. Prolonged heating can cause paper to burn. Napkins and kitchen towels should be white and unpatterned since any pattern or colour could be transferred to the food. Kitchen paper is used to absorb moisture and fat, for instance when reheating bakery items, and when cooking bacon. Greaseproof paper can be used as a loose covering, but avoid using waxed paper since the wax can melt from the heat of the food. Unless specially labelled for use in microwave ovens, plastic-coated paper plates should not be used.

Plastics

With the ever-increasing range of plastic ware available on the market, it is advisable to follow the manufacturer's recommendations, or test the containers as already explained. Several ranges of special microwave cookware are now available. Rigid plastic containers which are labelled 'dishwasher safe' or 'boilable' can normally be used for low-temperature short-term cooking. They should not, however, be used to heat or cook foods with a high fat or sugar content, e.g. butter, syrup or chocolate, which could damage the plastic or cause distortion.

Do not use lightweight plastic containers such as empty yoghurt or cottage cheese cartons which will be melted by the heat from the food. Plastic wrap or clingfilm is widely used in microwave cooking since it forms a good tight seal when food is to be covered. It should be pierced or slit at the end of the cooking period to avoid steam burns when it is removed from a container. Pierced roasting bags can be used to cook joints of meat, poultry and vegetables. Do not use the metal ties provided, but use string or an elastic band instead. Plastic cooking pouches containing commercially prepared foods can be slit on top, placed on an ovenproof plate without metal trim or in an ovenproof dish, and defrosted or cooked in the oven. Heatproof plastic spatulas, recommended for use in microwave ovens, are ideal for stirring and mixing.

Wicker, straw and wood

Wicker and straw baskets, without wire or staples, can be used for short-term heating only, e.g. for heating bread rolls. Wooden spoons can be left in the oven for short periods, for instance when making sauces; but if they have absorbed fat or moisture they will get hot. The moisture in wood evaporates during prolonged cooking and this can result in cracking.

Metal

Metal containers and utensils should never be used in a microwave oven. China and glass, or dishes with metal trim or manufacturer's mark in silver or gold on the base are also unsuitable, as is lead crystal or any material containing metal. This is because metal reflects microwave energy, inhibits cooking and can damage the magnetron. Foil-lined containers should not be used, and commercially frozen food in foil containers should be turned out into an ovenproof dish. Never place a can of food in the oven; always turn the contents into a suitable bowl or dish. Remove foil wrappings from products such as butter and cream cheese. In the same way as the metal twist-ties supplied with roasting bags should be replaced by string or elastic bands, wooden skewers or cocktail sticks should replace metal skewers when trussing poultry. Provided your manufacturer's instructions allow, you can use small smooth pieces of aluminium foil to shield the bone ends and wing tips of poultry, or the narrow ends of meat and fish, for part of the cooking time, to prevent overcooking in these areas. Foil must never touch any part of the oven interior.

Specially designed for the microwave oven

There is now a wide variety of both disposable and durable containers and utensils available on the market. Many can also be used in conventional ovens and home freezers. Follow the manufacturer's use and care instructions.

Microwave browning dishes These dishes have

a special coating on the base which absorbs microwave energy. The empty dish is preheated in the oven until the bottom surface becomes very hot. Food placed on the hot surface is sealed and browned while being cooked by microwave energy. Food is turned over during cooking to brown the second side. A browning dish is useful for cooking steaks, chops, sausages, burgers, crumbed foods and for baking scones.

Microwave roasting racks Specially designed roasting racks are now available. These are used to raise meats and poultry out of their own juices during cooking. They are also useful for reheating bakery products such as bread, bread rolls and pastry items, to prevent moist or soggy bases.

Thermometers There are specially designed thermometers for use in microwave cooking. Conventional meat and sugar thermometers must not be used in the oven but can, of course, be used after the food has been removed from the oven.

Measuring ingredients

The recipes in this book have been tested using both metric and imperial measures. It is important to weigh and measure accurately. The exact metric equivalent of the imperial 1oz is 28.35g, but the accepted equivalent is 25g. This means that the total volume of cooked food can vary slightly, depending on whether imperial or metric measurements are used. For this reason it is essential to follow either all imperial or all metric measurements; never mix the two. All spoon measures are level.

Length

Imperial	Metric Equivalent
½in	1.25cm
1in	2.5cm
6in	15cm
7in	17.5cm
8in	20cm
9in	22.5cm
10in	25cm

Weight

Imperial	Accepted Metric Equivalent	Exact Metric Equivalent
1oz	25g	28.35g
2oz	50g	56.7g
3oz	75g	85.05g
4oz	100g	113.4g
5oz	125g	141.75g
6oz	150g	170.1g
7oz	175g	198.45g
8oz	225g	226.8g
9oz	250g	255.15g
10oz	275g	283.5g
11oz	300g	311.85g
12oz	350g	340.2g
13oz	375g	368.54g
14oz	400g	396.9g
15oz	425g	425.24g
16oz (1lb)	450g	453.6g

Measuring spoon sizes

Imperial	Metric Equivalent
½ teaspoon (tsp)	2.5ml
1 teaspoon (tsp)	5ml
1 tablespoon (tbsp)	15ml

Volume

Imperial	Accepted Metric Equivalent	Exact Metric Equivalent
1fl oz	30ml	28.41ml
¼pt	150ml	142.06ml
½pt	300ml	284.12ml
¾pt	450ml	426.19ml
1pt	600ml	568.25ml

Defrosting

One of the greatest advantages of a microwave oven must surely be its ability to defrost frozen food in such a short time, compared with conventional methods. Used in conjunction with a home freezer it certainly comes into its own, and overcomes the need to remember to take food from the freezer the day before it is required. Most ovens today have a DEFROST or LOW setting, but power levels vary from one model to another. The setting used for defrosting in this book is referred to as LOW, with a power output level of 30 per cent on 650W ovens. If necessary, adjust times for higher or lower percentage outputs. The times given in defrosting charts throughout this book should be used as a guide only, and can vary, depending on the temperature at which the frozen food was stored in the freezer, as well as the efficiency of the microwave oven.

Useful hints:

1 Always underestimate the time taken to defrost food. If left for too long in the oven, it will start to cook.
2 Do not try to defrost foods completely in the microwave oven, otherwise they will start to cook around the outside. The defrosting process will finish during the standing time.
3 Remove lids from jars and containers. Slit plastic pouches or packets.
4 If food has to be placed in an ovenproof dish, match the size and shape of the dish to the size and shape of the food.
5 Remove metal ties from bags, and replace with string or an elastic band.
6 Joints of meat and poultry should be turned over during defrosting. Smaller items such as chops and bacon slices should be separated and rearranged as they defrost.
7 Frozen blocks of food should be gently broken up as they defrost and the still-frozen portions moved towards the outside of the dish.
8 Frozen fruit should be shaken or gently stirred during defrosting, and should be removed from the oven while still icy in the centre. It will thaw completely during the standing time.
9 Check food at the shortest time given. Different brands and weights may vary slightly.
10 Pour off excess liquid when defrosting poultry, since this absorbs microwave energy and slows down the process.

Guide to defrosting some everyday and convenience foods

Food	Quantity	Approximate Time on LOW Setting	Special Instructions
Bread			
loaf	1 large	7–8 min	Wrap in kitchen paper; turn over during defrosting
	1 small	4–6 min	Stand for 10 min
slice	1×25g (1oz)	10–15 sec	Place on kitchen paper
rolls	2	15–20 sec	Place on kitchen paper; stand for 2–3 min
Cakes			
dairy cream éclairs	4	1–1½ min	Remove from packaging; place on kitchen paper; stand 20 min
dairy cream sponge	1×6 portion	1½ min	Remove from packaging; place on kitchen paper; stand 20–25 min
dairy cream doughnuts	3	1 min	Remove from packaging; place on kitchen paper; stand 15 min
fruit topped cheesecake	1×6 portion	4 min	Remove from packaging; place on kitchen paper; stand 20–30 min
mince pies, cooked	4	1–1¼ min	Place on kitchen paper; stand 5 min

Food	Quantity	Approximate Time on LOW Setting	Special Instructions
Miscellaneous			
butter or margarine	250g (8.82oz) pack	1½–1¾ min	Remove wrapper; place on non-metallic plate; stand 5 min
mousse	1 individual	30 sec	Remove lid; stand 15–20 min
pastry	368g (13oz) pack	2 min	Defrost in pack
	212g (7½oz) pack	1 min	Stand 20–30 min
trifle	1 individual	1 min	Remove lid; stand 15–20 min

Guides to defrosting fish, meat and poultry, and fruit are to be found under their particular sections.

Reheating

Food reheated in a microwave oven looks and tastes as if it has been freshly cooked. Many foods in fact benefit from reheating. For example, casseroles and curries have more flavour if they are cooked the day before they are required, cooled and refrigerated overnight, and reheated the following day. Food can be cooked, when convenient, during the day and reheated at mealtimes. A meal for the latecomer can be pre-plated ready to reheat on arrival.

Useful hints:

1 Cover foods which should be kept moist, and add gravy or a sauce to sliced cold meat before reheating. Thinly sliced meat will heat more evenly than thickly sliced.
2 Arrange food in even layers, avoiding mounds of food which result in uneven heating.
3 When pre-plating a main course for the latecomer, arrange food in an even layer with thicker denser foods around the outside of the plate and less dense, quicker heating foods in the centre.
4 Do not overheat food. Feel the centre base of the dish or plate. If this is hot, the food has been heated sufficiently and is ready to eat.
5 Stir casseroles and vegetable dishes for even heating. Do not overheat already cooked jacket potatoes or they will dehydrate. Similarly, the fibrous stems of broccoli or asparagus spears will toughen if overheated.
6 When planning to reheat food, it is advisable to undercook it initially.
7 Food taken straight from the refrigerator will take longer to reheat than food at room temperature.
8 Arrange bread and bread products on absorbent kitchen paper to absorb moisture. Do not overheat, or they will toughen. Reheating requires only a few seconds.

Times given throughout this book for reheating food were tested on 650W ovens. If necessary, adjust times for ovens with higher or lower output. Times may vary depending on the starting temperature of the food and the efficiency of the microwave oven.

Guide to reheating non-frozen cooked and canned foods

Food	Quantity or Weight	Approximate Time on HIGH Setting	Special Instructions
Baked beans (canned)	219g (7¾oz) 447g (15¾oz)	1–1½ min 2–3 min	Turn into covered bowl; stir once during heating
Beef, sliced with gravy	1 serving 4 servings	1–2 min 3–5 min	Place on covered non-metallic plate or dish
Beverages (coffee, cocoa)	1×225g (8oz) mug 2×225g (8oz) mugs	1½–2 min 2½–3 min	Stir before serving
Casserole or stew	4 servings	8–10 min	Cover and stir during heating
Chicken portions	1×225g (8oz) 4×225g (8oz)	1½–2 min 5–7 min	Cover and rearrange during heating
Christmas pudding	450g (1lb) 900g (2lb)	up to 2 min up to 2½ min	Cover with plastic wrap; *do not overheat*; stand 2–3 min before serving

Food	Quantity or Weight	Approximate Time on HIGH Setting	Special Instructions
Fruit pie	1 portion	30 sec	Place on non-metallic serving plate
Garden peas (canned)	425g (15oz)	2–3 min	Turn into covered bowl; stir during heating
Hot dogs (in rolls)	2 4	45–50 sec 1–1½ min	Place on kitchen paper; *do not overheat*
Macaroni cheese (canned)	425g (15oz)	2½–3 min	Turn into covered bowl; stir during heating
Milk puddings (canned)	435g (15½oz)	2½–3 min	Turn into covered bowl; stir during heating
Mince pies	1 4	5–10 sec 20–30 sec	Place on kitchen paper; *do not overheat*; stand 2 min
Pre-plated main course	1	1½–2 min	Cover with plastic wrap; rotate if necessary during heating
Rice, long grain (refrigerated)	4 servings	3–4 min	Place with 2 tablespoons water in covered casserole; stir during heating
Soup, canned	425g (15oz)	3–4 min	Turn into covered bowl; stir during heating
Spaghetti in tomato sauce (canned)	435g (15½oz)	2½–3½ min	Turn into covered bowl; stir during heating
Sponge pudding (canned)	298g (10½oz)	1–1½ min	Remove from can; place on serving plate; cover with plastic wrap
Tomatoes (canned)	397g (14oz)	2–3 min	Turn into covered bowl; stir during heating
Vegetables	225g (8oz) 450g (1lb)	2 min 3–4 min	Place in covered bowl with 2tbsp water; stir during heating

Recipe Section

First steps

Although you are eager to use your new micro-wave oven, don't try to be too ambitious too soon. In other words don't attempt to cook a complete meal the first time you use the oven. To begin with try to cook only one dish at each meal by microwave, and continue to cook other foods as you normally do. Allow time to appreciate how quickly foods heat and cook by starting with simple things. Invite the family to join in too. Make a cup of coffee, cook a jacket potato, try scrambling eggs or cooking bacon. The recipes in this section are all quick and easy to prepare and cook and will give you confidence in using your new oven.

Instant tea *(serves 1)*

1 teabag
180ml (6fl oz) cold water
sugar, milk or lemon to taste

1 Place teabag in a cup without metal trim.
2 Pour in the water and microwave on HIGH for $1\frac{3}{4}$ min or until just boiling.
3 Remove teabag and add sugar, milk or lemon to taste.

Note: *2 cups will require about $3\frac{1}{4}$ min. Larger quantities are best made conventionally.*

Instant coffee *(serves 1)*

180ml (6fl oz) cold water
1×5ml tsp (1 tsp) instant coffee powder or granules
sugar, milk or cream to taste

1 Measure water into a cup or mug without metal trim.
2 Microwave on HIGH for $1\frac{3}{4}$ min or until just boiling.
3 Stir in coffee powder or granules and add sugar, milk or cream as preferred.

Note:
1 *2 cups will require approx $3\frac{1}{4}$ min. Larger quantities are best made conventionally.*
2 *Use milk instead of water. Heat 1 cup of milk for approx $1\frac{1}{2}$ min and 2 cups of milk for approx $2\frac{1}{2}$ min, to prevent boiling and spillage.*

Instant gaelic coffee *(serves 1)*

180ml (6fl oz) water
1×5ml tsp (1 tsp) instant coffee powder or granules
1×5ml tsp (1 tsp) demerara sugar
2×15ml tbsp (2tbsp) whisky
1×15ml tbsp (1tbsp) whipping cream

1 Pour the water into an Irish coffee goblet or serving glass (not lead crystal) and microwave on HIGH for $1\frac{1}{2}$ min.
2 Stir in the coffee and sugar, stirring until dissolved. Add whisky.
3 Microwave on HIGH for a further 30 sec.
4 Carefully pour the cream over the back of a warm spoon to float on top of the coffee. If preferred, the cream can be whipped and spooned on top of the coffee.

VARIATIONS
Calypso coffee: replace whisky with 4tsp of Tia Maria and proceed as above.
Viennese coffee: use a cup without metal trim. Omit whisky and proceed as above. Top with 1 rounded tbsp of whipped cream and sprinkle with finely grated chocolate.

Hot chocolate *(serves 1)*

180ml (6fl oz) milk
3 × 5ml tsp (3tsp) drinking chocolate powder, or as directed on pack
sugar, if required

1 Measure the milk into a cup without metal trim and microwave on HIGH for $1\frac{1}{2}$ min until hot but not boiling.
2 Stir in the chocolate powder. Add sugar if preferred.

VARIATION
Chocolate deluxe: proceed as above. After step 2 float a marshmallow on top of the hot chocolate and heat on HIGH for a further 10–15 sec, during which time the marshmallow will puff up and soften. The marshmallow will slowly collapse when removed from the oven.

Hot cocoa *(serves 1)*

1 × 5ml tsp (1tsp) cocoa, or as directed on pack
sugar to taste
180ml (6fl oz) milk, or milk and water

1 Blend the cocoa and sugar with a little of the measured milk, or milk and water, in a cup without metal trim.
2 Stir in remaining liquid and microwave on HIGH for $1\frac{1}{2}$ min until steaming but not boiling.
3 Stir before serving.

VARIATION
As for Hot chocolate.

Bacon *(serves 1)*

2 rashers bacon

1 Snip the bacon rind and fat at regular intervals to prevent it curling during cooking.
2 Place the rashers on double thickness crumpled kitchen paper on a plate without metal trim. Cover lightly with kitchen paper to prevent spluttering.
3 Microwave on HIGH for 2–$2\frac{1}{2}$ min or until cooked as preferred. Do not overcook or the bacon will become brittle.
4 Remove paper immediately, to prevent sticking.

Note:
1 *When cooking larger quantities of bacon, overlap the fat with the lean, or place the rashers in a suitable shallow dish or on a microwave roasting rack in a dish to catch the fat. Cover lightly with kitchen paper and cook on HIGH allowing 4–$4\frac{1}{2}$ min for 4 rashers and 5–6 min for 6 rashers. Rearrange bacon rashers during the cooking period.*
2 *Cooking times may vary according to type, thickness and cure of bacon.*
3 *Bacon can also be cooked in a microwave browning dish. Follow manufacturer's instructions for preheating and cooking.*

Baked jacket potato *(serves 1)*

1 × 150g (6oz) potato
1 × 15ml tbsp (1tbsp) soured cream, optional
1 × 5ml tsp (1 tsp) chopped chives, optional
blue cheese dressing, optional

1 Wash and dry the potato. Prick the skin, using a fork.
2 Place on a piece of kitchen paper on the floor of the oven and microwave on HIGH for $2\frac{1}{2}$ min.
3 Turn the potato over and continue cooking on HIGH for a further $2\frac{1}{2}$ min.
4 Wrap in foil, shiny side in, and leave to stand for 3–5 min to finish cooking before serving.

Baked jacket potatoes topped with sour cream and chives and blue cheese dressing (above); Ham steaks with pineapple (page 25); Broad beans; Bacon cooked on a microwave roasting rack (above)

5 If liked, remove foil after the standing time and cut a cross in the top of the potato. Squeeze the potato to push up the flesh. Top with either the soured cream and chives, or blue cheese dressing.

Note:

1 *When cooking more than one at a time, leave a 2.5cm (1in) space between each potato and arrange them in a circle on the floor of the oven. Remember to turn the potatoes over after half the total cooking time. Leave to stand as given above.*
2 × 150g (6oz) potatoes will require 7½–8 min total cooking time.
4 × 150g (6oz) potatoes will require 12–14 min total cooking time.
2 *Potatoes will feel firm when taken from the oven but will soften during the standing time. Do not overcook potatoes or they will dehydrate.*
3 *Cooked potatoes, wrapped in foil, will retain their heat for up to 30 min.*

Breakfast on a plate *(serves 1)*

2 rashers bacon, de-rinded if preferred
1 egg, at room temperature

1 Snip the bacon fat at regular intervals to prevent curling during cooking.
2 Arrange the bacon rashers around the outside of an ovenproof plate without metal trim.
3 Cover with kitchen paper and microwave on HIGH for 1½–1¾ min until almost cooked. Turn the bacon over.
4 Break the egg into a saucer, pierce the yolk carefully with a fork and slide into the centre of the plate.
5 Cover with plastic wrap and microwave on HIGH for 45–60 sec, depending on size of egg used. Do not overcook.
6 Leave to stand, covered, for 2 min to finish cooking before serving.

Mulled wine *(makes 750ml/1¼pt)*

750ml (1¼pt) red wine
1 cinnamon stick
3 × 15ml tbsp (3tbsp) sugar
pinch of nutmeg
fresh orange slices

1 Place all the ingredients, except orange slices, in a suitable 1.5 litre (3pt) bowl.
2 Microwave on HIGH for 5 min, stirring once during heating.
3 Serve hot with orange slices floating on top.

Three-minute soup *(serves 1)*

300ml (½pt) soup, home-made or canned

1 Pour the soup into a serving bowl or mug without metal trim.
2 Microwave on HIGH for 3 min, stirring once during heating.

Note: *2 bowls or mugs of soup will require approx 5 min to reach serving temperature.*

Porridge *(serves 1)*

25g (1oz) porridge oats
240ml (8fl oz) water, or milk and water
pinch of salt

1 Stir all the ingredients together in a cereal bowl without metal trim.
2 Microwave on HIGH for 2–2½ min until porridge has boiled and thickened. Stir once during cooking and at the end of the cooking period.
3 Leave to stand for 1–2 min before serving either with extra salt or sugar and milk or cream.

Note: *For 3 servings place 75g (3oz) porridge oats with 750ml (1¼pt) water or milk and water and a good pinch of salt into a suitable bowl or casserole. Cover and microwave on HIGH for about 6 min, stirring once during cooking and at the end of the cooking period. Leave to stand for 2–3 min before serving as above.*

Heating bread rolls

Place the required number of room-temperature bread rolls on absorbent kitchen paper. If heating more than 2, arrange them in a circle.

Microwave on HIGH:
1 roll 10–15 sec, depending on size
2 rolls 15–20 sec, depending on size
4 rolls 20–25 sec, depending on size.
Leave to stand for a few seconds to distribute heat.

VARIATION
Frozen bread rolls can be heated in the same way, allowing the following times on HIGH:
1 roll 15–20 sec, depending on size
2 rolls 20–25 sec, depending on size
4 rolls 25–30 sec, depending on size.

Scrambled eggs (serves 1)

15g ($\frac{1}{2}$oz) butter, optional
2 eggs
2×15ml tbsp (2tbsp) milk
salt and pepper
bread, toasted conventionally
butter

1 Melt the butter, if used, in an ovenproof bowl or jug on HIGH for 30 sec.
2 Beat the eggs and milk together, add seasoning, and stir into melted butter.
3 Microwave on HIGH for 1½–2 min, depending on size of eggs used and preferred consistency. Stir every 30 sec. Do not overcook (see Note).
4 Stand for about a minute to finish cooking.
5 Serve on hot buttered toast.

Note:
1 *Remove eggs from the oven while they are still soft and moist. If after standing they are not cooked sufficiently for your liking, simply return them to the oven and cook on HIGH for a further 10–15 sec. Stir before serving.*
2 *For 2 servings use 4 eggs and 4tbsp milk. Proceed as above and cook for about 3 min.*

Ham steaks with pineapple (serves 2)

2×100g (4oz) ham steaks
2 slices fresh or canned pineapple
watercress

1 Arrange the ham steaks in a shallow ovenproof dish or on an ovenproof plate without metal trim.
2 Cover with plastic wrap and microwave on HIGH for 3 min.
3 Turn the steaks over and place a pineapple ring on top of each.
4 Microwave, uncovered, on HIGH for a further 2 min. Do not overcook.
5 Leave to stand covered for 2 min to finish cooking, before serving garnished with watercress.

Chocolate marshmallow delights (makes 6)

6 digestive biscuits
2×25g (1oz) bars thin milk chocolate
6 pink or white marshmallows
6 chocolate digestive biscuits

1 Arrange the plain digestive biscuits in a circle on kitchen paper on a plate without metal trim, or on the floor of the oven.
2 Place one-third of a bar of chocolate on each biscuit.
3 Top with a marshmallow.
4 Microwave on HIGH for 45–60 sec until the marshmallows have puffed up. *Do not overheat.*
5 Top with a chocolate digestive biscuit, chocolate side uppermost.
6 Leave to stand for 1 min to allow heat from the marshmallow to melt the chocolate. Serve immediately.

Note: *Marshmallows have a high sugar content and will scorch in the centre if overheated. The marshmallows heat first, and the chocolate melts during the standing time. Do not leave in the oven till the chocolate melts or the marshmallows will be scorched.*

VARIATION
Omit the chocolate filling and proceed as above.

Custard sauce *(makes 300ml/½pt)*

1 × 15ml tbsp (1tbsp) custard powder
1 × 15ml tbsp (1tbsp) sugar
300ml (½pt) milk

1 Blend the custard powder and sugar with a little of the measured milk, in a Pyrex or suitable jug.
2 Gradually stir in the remaining milk.
3 Microwave on HIGH for 3½–4 min until sauce has boiled and thickened. Stir every minute.

Note: *To make 600ml (1pt) of custard, double the above quantities, use a large jug at least 1 litre (1¾pt) capacity to prevent spillage, and cook on HIGH for about 6 min.*

VARIATIONS
Substitute cornflour or flavoured blancmange powder for custard powder and proceed as above.

Stewed apples *(makes 450g/1lb)*

450g (1lb) prepared weight of cooking apples, thinly sliced
1 × 15ml tbsp (1tbsp) sugar, or to taste
1 × 15ml tbsp (1tbsp) water

1 Place the prepared apples in an ovenproof casserole with the sugar and water.
2 Cover with a lid of plastic wrap and micro-wave on HIGH for 2½ min.
3 Stir, re-cover and cook for about a further 2½ min, depending on cooking quality of apples used.
4 Leave to stand for 2 min before serving.

Compôte of dried fruit *(serves 5–6)*

450ml (¾pt) water
350g (12oz) mixed dried fruit (prunes, apricots etc)
25g (1oz) brown sugar
2 × 5ml tsp (2tsp) grated lemon rind
1 × 15ml tbsp (1tbsp) brandy, optional

1 Place water and fruit in a large bowl.

2 Cover with plastic wrap and microwave on HIGH for 6 min.
3 Stir in remaining ingredients.
4 Re-cover and microwave on HIGH for a further 8 min.
5 Leave to stand, covered, for 30 min, to re-hydrate.
6 Refrigerate, covered, for several hours, or overnight, before serving.

Note: *If softer fruit is preferred, soak the fruit in water for a few hours before cooking.*

Baked stuffed apple *(serves 1)*

1 medium-sized cooking apple
2–3 × 5ml tsp (2–3tsp) mincemeat

1 Wash and dry the apple. Remove the core, prick the skin all over with a fork and place on a plate or in an individual serving dish without metal trim.
2 Fill the cavity with mincemeat. Cover loosely with greased greaseproof paper.
3 Microwave on HIGH for 2½–3 min, depending on size. Apple should still be firm when removed from the oven.
4 Leave to stand, covered, for 2 min, to finish cooking.
5 Spoon juice over apple before serving.

Note:
1 *The speed of cooking may vary with the type, as well as the size, of apple used.*
2 *When cooking more than 1 apple at a time, leave a space of 2.5cm (1in) between each, and arrange 3 or more in a circle around the outside of a suitable shallow round dish.*

VARIATIONS
Vary the filling by replacing the mincemeat with mixed dried fruit, dates, dates and nuts. Or simply fill the centres with brown sugar, topped with a knob of butter and sprinkled with cin-namon, if liked.

Compôte of dried fruit (above); Baked apples stuffed with mincemeat (above)

Snacks

Again, this section is intended to allow you to become familiar with your oven before you try to cook main course dishes. Hot snacks are quick and easy to prepare and can be heated so quickly in a microwave oven. Every member of the family can prepare his or her own favourite snack in just a few minutes. The children can heat their own baked beans, and father may like to make his own bacon sandwich. Bread is toasted conventionally, of course, using either the grill of a conventional cooker or an electric toaster, and at the same time the snack filling or topping will be heating or cooking in the micro-wave oven. Never overheat bread, for example when preparing hot dogs or hamburgers, otherwise it will become tough. Look as you cook, and don't overcook.

Ring-around frankfurters *(serves 1)*

2 frankfurters
3 × 15 ml tbsp (3 tbsp) baked beans
dash of Worcestershire sauce, optional
tomato ketchup or barbecue sauce

1 Make deep slits in the outside edge of the frankfurters at 1.25 cm ($\frac{1}{2}$ in) intervals.
2 Arrange the slit frankfurters on a serving plate, without metal trim, the slit sides towards the outside.
3 Form into circles, securing the ends together with wooden cocktail sticks.
4 Mix the baked beans with the Worcestershire sauce, if used, and spoon into the centre of the frankfurters.
5 Brush the frankfurters with tomato ketchup or barbecue sauce.
6 Microwave on HIGH for $1\frac{3}{4}$ min or until hot.

VARIATIONS
Substitute canned spaghetti in tomato sauce or macaroni cheese for the baked beans, and proceed as above.

Sausage and bean casserole *(serves 4)*

450 g (1 lb) thick pork sausages at room temperature
1 × 450 g (15.9 oz) can barbecue beans or curried beans with sultanas

1 Prick the sausages all over with a fork and place in an ovenproof casserole.
2 Cover loosely with kitchen paper and micro-wave on HIGH for $3\frac{1}{2}$ min.
3 Turn the sausages over and rearrange their position in the dish. Pour off any fat.
4 Re-cover and continue cooking on HIGH for a further 3 min. Pour off any fat.
5 Add the beans to the casserole, cover with a lid or plastic wrap and microwave on HIGH for $3\frac{1}{2}$ min, stirring once during this time.
6 For a more substantial quick snack, serve over toasted bread or accompanied by instant potato made up acccording to packet instructions.

Note: *If preferred, sausages can be cooked in a microwave browning dish, following manufacturer's instructions for preheating and cooking times.*

Cheesy baked beans on toast (serves 1)

1 × 150g (5.3oz) can baked beans
1 thick slice of bread, toasted conventionally
  and buttered if preferred
1 × 15ml tbsp (1tbsp) mature cheddar cheese,
  grated
paprika

1 Place beans in a small ovenproof bowl.
2 Cover with plastic wrap and microwave on
   HIGH for 1 min.
3 Place the toast on a serving plate, without
   metal trim, and top with the beans.
4 Sprinkle with the cheese and microwave on
   HIGH for 30 sec or until the cheese has started
   to melt.
5 Stand for 1 min before serving, sprinkled
   with paprika.

Note: *To reduce washing up, beans may be
placed on the toast before heating. Cover
loosely with a small piece of greaseproof paper
and microwave on* HIGH *for 1½ min. Top with
cheese and continue heating on* HIGH *for a
further 30 sec or until cheese starts to melt.*

VARIATION
Substitute a small can of spaghetti for the baked
beans.

Tomato, cheese and onion crisp (serves 3)

350g (12oz) tomatoes, skinned and sliced
1 medium onion, peeled and grated
75g (3oz) grated cheese, preferably Gruyère
salt
cayenne pepper
1 × 25g (1oz) pkt cheese and onion crisps,
  crushed

1 Grease a shallow ovenproof dish.
2 Arrange a layer of sliced tomatoes in the bottom of the dish and cover with a layer of
   onion and cheese, seasoning each layer.
3 Repeat layers.
4 Cover with plastic wrap and cook on HIGH for
   5 min.
5 Sprinkle with crushed crisps and heat on HIGH
   for 1 min.

Herring roes on toast (serves 2)

150g (6oz) soft herring roes
25g (1oz) butter
salt and pepper
2 slices bread, toasted conventionally and
  buttered if preferred
lemon wedges
chopped parsley

1 Wash the roes and pat dry on kitchen paper.
2 Place the butter in a shallow ovenproof dish
   and microwave on HIGH for 1 min.
3 Arrange the roes in an even layer in the dish
   and cover with plastic wrap.
4 Microwave on HIGH for 1½ min.
5 Turn the roes over, re-cover and cook on
   HIGH for a further 1 min.
6 Season to taste and serve on the toast accompanied by lemon wedges and sprinkled with
   chopped parsley.

Sardines on toast (serves 1)

1 × 120g (4½oz) can sardines, drained
lemon juice, optional
2 slices bread, toasted conventionally and
  buttered if preferred
1 tomato, skinned and sliced

1 If preferred, the sardines may first be boned
   and mashed with a little lemon juice.
2 Place the toast on a serving plate, without
   metal trim, and arrange or spread the sardines on it.
3 Top with tomato slices and microwave on
   HIGH for 1½ min.

Note: *For 2 servings, double the above quantities and microwave on* HIGH *for about 2½ min.*

VARIATION
Substitute mackerel for sardines.

Hot dogs *(makes 4)*

1 medium onion, peeled and chopped
1×15ml tbsp (1tbsp) water
4 soft finger rolls
4 frankfurters
tomato or other relish

1 Place the onion and water in an ovenproof bowl.
2 Cover with plastic wrap and microwave on HIGH for 3 min, stirring or shaking after 1½ min. Drain cooked onion.
3 Split the rolls in half lengthways and place a frankfurter with some cooked onion in each one.
4 Arrange on kitchen paper on a plate without metal trim, or on the floor of the oven.
5 Cover with kitchen paper and microwave on HIGH for 2 min, rearranging the hot dogs after 1 min.
6 Serve topped with favourite relish.

Note:

1 *1 hot dog will only need heating for about 40 sec on* HIGH; *2 hot dogs will require about 1 min.*
2 *The hot dogs can be individually wrapped, ready to serve, in paper napkins. Use only white, not coloured, napkins to prevent transfer of colour.*

Hamburgers *(makes 4 large)*

450g (1lb) lean beef, finely minced
1 small onion, peeled and grated, optional
1×5ml tsp (1tsp) mixed dried herbs, optional
salt and pepper
4 burger buns or soft round baps

1 Mix together the minced beef, onion and herbs if used. Add seasoning.
2 Divide mixture into 4 and form into flat rounds of size to fit inside the buns or baps.
3 Arrange the rounds on a microwave roasting rack in a dish, or in a circle on kitchen paper on a large plate, without metal trim.
4 Cover loosely with greaseproof paper and microwave on HIGH for 3½ min.

5 Turn burgers over, rearrange, re-cover and continue cooking on HIGH for 3 min or until burgers are cooked as preferred. Leave to stand, covered, for 2–3 min.
6 Split the buns or baps and place a burger in each.
7 Arrange them in a circle on kitchen paper on a plate or on the floor of the oven and heat on HIGH for about 1 min.
8 Serve with mustards and burger relishes on a bed of lettuce, garnished with tomato and onion or chives.

VARIATION
Cheeseburgers: proceed as above to step 6. Top each burger with a slice of cheese, and onion if liked, before heating on HIGH as above for 1–1½ min until cheese has started to melt. Stand for 1–2 min before serving.

Browning dish cheese sandwich *(serves 2)*

4 sandwich slices processed cheese, plain or
  with onion
4 slices bread
butter

1 Preheat microwave browning dish according to manufacturer's instructions.
2 Meanwhile place 2 slices of cheese between each 2 slices of bread, and butter the outside of the sandwiches on both sides.
3 Using oven gloves, remove the dish from the oven and place on a protected work surface.
4 Place the sandwiches immediately on the base of the preheated dish and flatten them with a palette knife to ensure overall contact with the hot base.
5 Leave the sandwiches for 20–30 sec until brown underneath.
6 Turn over, preferably onto another unused part of the heated base. Press down as before and leave for a further 30–45 sec to brown the second side.
7 If necessary, return the sandwiches in the dish to the oven and microwave on HIGH for 15–30 sec to finish melting the cheese.

Hot dogs and relish (above); Hamburgers (above); Browning dish cheese sandwiches (above)

Note:

1 *Work surfaces must be protected from the heat of the browning dish.*
2 *The sandwiches are browned in the dish outside the oven.*

VARIATIONS

1 Spread pickle, mustard or ketchup between the cheese slices.
2 Fill sandwiches with 1 thin slice of ham and 1 slice of cheese.
3 Use unprocessed cheese, cut into thin slices.

Supper savoury *(serves 4)*

4 rashers bacon, without rind
100g (4oz) mature Cheddar cheese, grated
2×15ml tbsp (2tbsp) plain flour
salt and pepper
675g (1½lb) potatoes, peeled and thinly sliced
2 medium tomatoes, skinned and sliced
300ml (½pt) milk
25g (1oz) butter
paprika

1 Place bacon on an ovenproof plate, cover with kitchen paper and microwave on HIGH for 3½–4 min until crisp.
2 Crumble the bacon into a bowl, stir in the cheese, flour and seasoning.
3 Place half the sliced potatoes in the bottom of a 1.4 litre (2½pt) ovenproof pie dish or casserole.
4 Top with half the tomatoes and then with half the bacon and cheese mixture.
5 Repeat these layers, ending with the bacon and cheese mixture.
6 Measure the milk into a heatproof jug, microwave on HIGH for 2 min and pour into the dish.
7 Flake the butter on top and sprinkle with paprika.
8 Microwave on HIGH for 15 min or until potatoes are cooked.

Welsh rarebit *(serves 1–2)*

100g (4oz) mature Cheddar cheese, grated
½×5ml tsp (½tsp) mustard powder
pepper
dash of Worcestershire sauce, optional
2×15ml tbsp (2tbsp) milk or brown ale
2 slices bread, toasted conventionally

1 Place the cheese, mustard, pepper, Worcestershire sauce if used, and milk or ale in an ovenproof bowl.
2 Microwave on HIGH for 30 sec.
3 Stir well and microwave on HIGH for a further 15–30 sec, until cheese has melted.
4 Stir well and spread over the toast.
5 Brown under a preheated conventional grill before serving.

VARIATION
Proceed as above to step 4. Top with bacon rashers and cook under a preheated conventional grill.

Toasted bacon sandwich *(serves 1)*

2–3 bacon rashers
2 slices bread, toasted conventionally

1 De-rind bacon if preferred. Snip into fat at regular intervals to prevent curling.
2 Arrange bacon on an ovenproof plate and cover loosely with kitchen paper.
3 Microwave on HIGH for 2–3 min, depending on quantity used and whether preferred medium or well done. Do not overcook, or bacon will be brittle.
4 Brush one side of the toasted bread with the melted bacon fat before making the sandwich.
5 If hot sandwich is preferred, place the sandwich on a piece of kitchen paper or white napkin on a serving plate without metal trim, and reheat on HIGH for 30 sec before serving.

VARIATION
Use untoasted bread, or bread toasted on one side only, and proceed as above.

Hawaiian open sandwich *(serves 2)*

2 thick slices bread, toasted conventionally
2 slices ham
2 pineapple rings, fresh or canned
50g (2oz) grated cheese
paprika

1 Place the toast on kitchen paper on a plate without metal trim.
2 Top each slice of toast with a slice of ham, and a pineapple ring.
3 Sprinkle with grated cheese and microwave on HIGH for 1½–2 min until cheese has melted and sandwiches are just warm. Do not overheat.
4 Sprinkle with paprika before serving.

Muffin pizzas *(serves 2–4)*

2 plain or cheese muffins
1×227g (8oz) can tomatoes, drained and chopped
good pinch of mixed herbs or pizza seasoning
1×15ml tbsp (1 tbsp) grated onion
salt and pepper
75g (3oz) grated cheese, preferably mozzarella
anchovy fillets and olives to garnish, optional

1 Split the muffins and arrange the 4 halves in a circle on kitchen paper, on a plate without metal trim.
2 Mix together the tomatoes, herbs or pizza seasoning, and onion. Add salt and pepper to taste.
3 Top the muffins with the mixture and sprinkle with cheese.
4 Microwave on HIGH for 2½ min or until cheese has melted.
5 Garnish if liked with anchovy fillets and olives before serving.

VARIATION
Place a slice of salami on the muffins before topping with the tomato mixture and cheese.

Pie and mushy peas *(serves 1)*

1 ready-cooked individual meat pie, at room temperature, weighing 125–150g (5–6oz)
1×290g (10½oz) can mushy peas

1 Remove foil container and place the pie on kitchen paper on a serving plate, without metal trim.
2 Cover loosely with kitchen paper.
3 Microwave on HIGH for 1½ min. Leave to stand.
4 Meanwhile empty half the contents of the can of peas into a small ovenproof bowl. Reserve remainder for future use.
5 Cover the bowl and heat the peas on HIGH for about 1 min.
6 Remove the kitchen paper from the pie and spoon the peas over.

Creamed mushrooms *(serves 2–3)*

25g (1oz) butter, flaked
225g (8oz) button mushrooms
1 tablespoon cornflour
300ml (½pt) full cream milk
2×15ml tbsp (2 tbsp) single or whipping cream
salt and pepper
squeeze of lemon juice
Parmesan cheese, optional

1 Place the butter and mushrooms in an ovenproof bowl.
2 Cover and microwave on HIGH for 3 min.
3 Blend the cornflour to a smooth paste with a little of the measured milk, in an ovenproof jug or bowl.
4 Stir in the remaining milk and the mushrooms with their juice.
5 Microwave on HIGH for 4 min or until sauce has boiled and thickened. Stir every minute.
6 Stir in the cream, season to taste, finally stir in the lemon juice.
7 Serve as a vegetable or on buttered toast, sprinkled with Parmesan cheese, if used.

Soups and starters

Save on washing up by heating or cooking soups and starters in the serving dish. An individual bowl or mug of soup is always welcome, especially on cold winter days, and can be heated in just 3 min. Always choose a large ovenproof soup tureen or bowl when cooking home-made soup, to prevent spillage. When a recipe calls for boiling stock, boil the water in an electric kettle and use a stock cube, if home-made stock is not available. Use your microwave oven to heat canned and packet soups.

How to heat canned soups

1×435g (15oz) can soup

Method:
1 Turn the soup into a 1 litre (1¾pt) ovenproof jug. Stir and cover with plastic wrap.
2 Microwave on HIGH for about 4 min, or until serving temperature is reached. Stir during heating.
3 Stir soup after removing from the oven, before serving.

Note: *To heat condensed canned soups, dilute with water as instructed by the manufacturer and proceed as above. One 275g (10oz) can, diluted with water, will require about 6 min to reach serving temperature.*

How to cook packet soups

1×600ml (1pt) or 900ml (1½pt) packet soup mix

Method:
1 Empty the packet of soup mix into a large ovenproof bowl and gradually stir in water, according to packet instructions.
2 Leave to stand and soak for about 30 min, to soften.
3 Cover with plastic wrap and microwave on HIGH until boiling; 600ml (1pt) will require about 6 min, 900ml (1½pt) about 8 min. Stir during heating.
4 Stir and continue cooking on HIGH for a further 2 min, or on LOW for a further 5 min.
5 Leave to stand for 3 min. Stir before serving.

Sherried grapefruit *(serves 4)*

2 large grapefruit
2×15ml tbsp (2tbsp) dry sherry
4×5ml tsp (4tsp) brown or demerara sugar
½×5ml tsp (½tsp) ground cinnamon, optional
2 maraschino cherries, drained and halved

1 Cut the grapefruit in half, or make a waterlily effect by cutting round it in points with scissors if preferred.
2 Remove pips, and segment with a grapefruit or serrated knife.
3 Place the fruit in individual ovenproof dishes, without metal trim.
4 Pour over the sherry and sprinkle with sugar and cinnamon. Leave to stand for about 30 min.
5 Arrange the dishes in a circle in the oven.
6 Microwave on HIGH for about 4 min until really hot.
7 Serve decorated with maraschino cherries.

Potato and watercress soup (page 36); Sherried grapefruit (above); Meatballs in tomato sauce (page 52)

Cocktail meatballs *(makes about 30)*

225g (8oz) lean minced beef
3 × 15ml tbsp (3tbsp) breadcrumbs or rolled
  oats
1 small onion, peeled and finely chopped
1 × 5ml tsp (1tsp) chopped parsley
1 × 15ml tbsp (1tbsp) tomato ketchup
beaten egg to bind
salt and pepper

1 Mix all the ingredients together and shape into small balls 1.8cm (¾in) in diameter.
2 Place meatballs, 15 at a time, in a single layer in a shallow round ovenproof dish.
3 Cover with plastic wrap and microwave on HIGH for 2 min.
4 Rearrange meatballs in dish, re-cover and microwave on LOW for 3 min, or until fully cooked.
5 Repeat steps 2 to 4 with remaining meatballs.
6 Serve hot or cold on cocktail sticks, with a dip.

Potato and watercress soup *(serves 4)*

25g (1oz) butter or margarine
1 medium onion, peeled and finely chopped
1 stick celery, chopped
1 bunch watercress
350g (12oz) prepared weight potatoes, diced
750ml (1¼pt) boiling chicken stock
salt and pepper
120ml (4fl oz) double cream

1 Place the butter or margarine in a 2.8 litre (5pt) ovenproof bowl and melt on HIGH for about 30 sec.
2 Stir in onion and celery. Cover and cook on HIGH for 2 min.
3 Meanwhile reserve a few watercress leaves to garnish, and chop the remaining leaves and stems finely.
4 Add the chopped watercress, potatoes, stock and seasoning to the onion and celery.
5 Cover and microwave on HIGH for 15 min.
6 Purée the soup in an electric blender or food processor and return to the rinsed bowl.
7 Stir in the cream and heat on HIGH for 2 min. Do not allow to boil.

8 Serve hot or cold, garnished with reserved watercress leaves, accompanied by crusty French bread.

French onion soup *(serves 4–6)*

450g (1lb) onions, peeled and thinly sliced
25g (1oz) butter or margarine
15g (½oz) cornflour
1.1 litre (2pt) boiling beef stock
salt and pepper
4–6 slices French bread, toasted conventionally
grated cheese
chopped parsley, optional

1 Place the onions with the butter or margarine in a large ovenproof bowl.
2 Cover and microwave on HIGH for 6 min. Stir twice during cooking.
3 Stir in the cornflour. Gradually blend in the stock and add seasoning.
4 Cover and microwave on HIGH for 20 min.
5 Turn into a large flameproof serving dish or individual flameproof soup bowls.
6 Float toasted bread on top, and sprinkle with grated cheese.
7 Heat in the microwave oven on HIGH for 3 min or until cheese is melted; having arranged individual bowls in a circle.
8 Alternatively brown the cheese under a pre-heated conventional grill.
9 Serve sprinkled with chopped parsley, if used.

Tomato soup *(serves 4–6)*

1 medium onion, peeled and finely chopped
1 clove garlic, peeled and crushed
750ml (1¼pt) tomato juice
1kg (2lb) ripe tomatoes, skinned, halved and
  de-seeded
salt and pepper
chopped chives

1 Place the onion and garlic with 300ml (½pt) of the tomato juice in an ovenproof bowl or casserole. Cover and microwave on HIGH for 5 min.

2 Roughly chop the tomatoes and add them with the remaining tomato juice to the onion mixture.

3 Cover and microwave on HIGH for a further 5 min.

4 Sieve or purée in an electric blender or food processor.

5 Season to taste and serve hot and cold, garnished with chopped chives.

Cream of cauliflower soup *(serves 4–5)*

25g (1oz) butter or margarine
450g (1lb) cauliflower florets
1 medium onion, peeled and finely chopped
2×5ml tsp (2tsp) cornflour
900ml (1½pt) boiling chicken stock
150ml (¼pt) milk or single cream
salt and pepper
2×15ml tbsp (2tbsp) finely chopped parsley
grated Parmesan cheese, optional

1 Place the butter or margarine, cauliflower and onion in a large 2.8 litre (5pt) ovenproof bowl.

2 Cover and microwave on HIGH for 10 min, stirring after 5 min.

3 Blend cornflour with a little cold water and gradually stir in the stock.

4 Stir this with the milk or cream into the vegetables.

5 Cover and microwave on HIGH for 10 min or until vegetables are soft.

6 Purée in an electric blender or food processor.

7 Return soup to rinsed bowl and season to taste.

8 Cover and heat on HIGH for about 3 min.

9 Stir in chopped parsley just before serving.

10 Serve with grated Parmesan cheese, if liked.

Cream of mushroom soup *(serves 4)*

50g (2oz) butter or margarine
225g (8oz) mushrooms, chopped
1 medium onion, peeled and finely chopped
25g (1oz) cornflour
300ml (½pt) boiling chicken stock
300ml (½pt) creamy milk
150ml (¼pt) single cream, optional
salt and pepper
a few thin mushroom slices to garnish

1 Place the butter or margarine, mushrooms and onion in a large ovenproof bowl.

2 Cover and cook on HIGH for 4 min, stirring after 2 min.

3 Blend the cornflour with a little cold water. Blend in the stock and add this to the mushroom mixture.

4 Blend in the milk, and cream if used.

5 Microwave on HIGH for 7 min, stirring after every 2 min.

6 Season to taste.

7 Either serve the soup as it is, or purée in an electric blender or food processor.

8 Garnish with a few thin slices of mushroom.

Lentil soup *(serves 4)*

100g (4oz) red lentils
1 medium onion, peeled and finely chopped
2 sticks celery, washed and finely chopped
1 medium-sized carrot, finely chopped
1×5ml tsp (1tsp) paprika
pinch of cayenne pepper
900ml (1½pt) boiling ham stock made from 2 ham stock cubes and water
salt and pepper
chopped parsley to garnish

1 Wash the lentils, pick them over for stones and soak for 2 hr. Drain.

2 Place the drained lentils, with remaining ingredients except parsley, in a large 2.8 litre (5pt) ovenproof bowl.

3 Cover with plastic wrap and microwave on HIGH for 10 min.

4 Stir well, re-cover and continue cooking on HIGH for a further 10 min or until lentils are tender.

5 Check seasoning and serve sprinkled with chopped parsley. Or, if preferred, purée the soup in an electric blender or food processor before serving.

Kipper pâté *(serves 4–6)*

2 × 198g (7oz) packs buttered kipper fillets
100g (4oz) cottage or curd cheese
2 × 15ml tbsp (2tbsp) natural unsweetened low
 fat yoghurt
pepper
cress to garnish

1 Place fish in a shallow ovenproof dish. Cover
 and microwave on HIGH for 9 min. Separate
 fillets after about 3 min, and rearrange after
 6 min.
2 Remove skin from fish and flake the flesh.
3 Stir in the cheese, yoghurt and pepper to
 taste.
4 Transfer mixture to an electric blender or
 food processor and blend till smooth.
5 Turn into individual dishes and refrigerate till
 set.
6 Serve garnished with cress, accompanied by
 Melba toast or freshly toasted wholemeal
 bread.

Chicken liver pâté with mushrooms
(serves 6)

1 medium onion, peeled and finely chopped
1 clove garlic, finely chopped
50g (2oz) butter, cut into small pieces
450g (1lb) chicken livers, sliced
salt
pinch of cayenne pepper
1 × 5ml tsp (1tsp) prepared mustard
1 × 15ml tbsp (1tbsp) double cream
3 × 15ml tbsp (3tbsp) brandy
1 × 213g (7½oz) can mushrooms in brine,
 drained
sliced stuffed olives, gherkin fans or juniper
 berries to garnish
lemon wedges

1 Place the onion, garlic and butter in a
 medium-sized ovenproof bowl.
2 Cover and microwave on HIGH for 3 min. Stir
 after 2 min.
3 Stir in sliced chicken livers.
4 Re-cover and cook on HIGH for about 7 min
 until livers are only just cooked. Do not overcook. Stir after 3½ min. Leave to cool slightly.

5 Stir in salt, cayenne, mustard, cream, brandy
 and mushrooms.
6 Transfer mixture to an electric blender or
 food processor and process until smooth.
7 Turn into a serving dish or individual dishes.
 Cool and refrigerate for at least 2 hr.
8 Garnish before serving with Melba toast,
 buttered brown bread or crusty French
 bread, and lemon wedges.

Devilled mushrooms *(serves 3)*

225g (8oz) button mushrooms, sliced
25g (1oz) butter, flaked
120ml (4fl oz) double cream
2 × 5ml tsp (2tsp) Worcestershire sauce
2 × 5ml tsp (2tsp) tomato ketchup
½ × 5ml tsp (2tsp) mustard powder
pinch of ground nutmeg
salt and pepper, if necessary
paprika or chopped parsley

1 Place the mushrooms with the butter in an
 ovenproof bowl.
2 Cover with plastic wrap and cook on HIGH for
 3¼ min, stirring after 2 min.
3 Blend together the cream, Worcestershire
 sauce, ketchup, mustard powder and nutmeg. Season only if necessary.
4 Gently stir in the mushrooms.
5 Divide the mixture among individual ovenproof dishes without metal trim.
6 Arrange the dishes in a circle in the oven.
7 Microwave on LOW for about 3 min or until
 heated through. Do not allow mixture to
 boil.
8 Stir gently and serve sprinkled with paprika
 or chopped parsley.

Soused herrings (page 41); Baked trout (page 42)

Fish

Fish cooked correctly in a microwave oven retains its natural juices and is full of flavour. Many non-fish eaters have been converted, and thoroughly enjoy fish cooked by microwave energy. Often the only addition necessary to produce an enjoyable main course is a knob of butter or a little lemon juice. Fish cooks very quickly, and must not be overcooked, otherwise it will become tough and dry. For this reason it is best not to reheat fish. If a fish dish must be reheated, plan to undercook it initially to allow for this, and reheat for the minimum amount of time.

Always cover fish during cooking except when cooking it on a microwave browning dish, and remember that, like other foods, it con-tinues to cook during the standing time. Arrange fish with the thicker parts towards the outside of the ovenproof cooking dish or plate, and cover narrow tail-ends with smooth pieces of aluminium foil if your oven manufacturer allows. Frozen fish is defrosted on LOW setting, and fillets or cutlets should be separated during defrosting. Large whole fish should have the skin slit diagonally in three places on both sides to prevent bursting during cooking. Whole fish and thick pieces of fish also benefit from turning over after half the cooking time. 'Boil-in-the-bag' commercially prepared fish should have the bag slit on top before cooking. Never attempt to deep-fat fry in a microwave oven.

Guide to defrosting fish

Fish	Quantity	Approximate Time on LOW Setting	Special Instructions
Fillets, cutlets, steaks	225g ($\frac{1}{2}$lb) 450g (1lb)	3–4 min 5–8 min	Cover and separate during defrosting; stand 5–10 min
Whole fish	450g (1lb)	6–8 min	Cover; turn over during defrosting; stand 5–10 min
Rainbow trout	1 × 175g (7oz)	3$\frac{1}{2}$ min	Slit pack and place on non-metallic plate; stand 5 min
Prawns	225g (8oz) 450g (1lb)	3–4 min 5–6 min	Slit pouch, flex during defrosting; stand 5 min
Kippers	225g (8oz) 450g (1lb)	3 min 4–6 min	Cover; separate during defrosting; stand 5 min

Guide to cooking fish

Fish	Quantity	Approximate Time on HIGH Setting	Special Instructions
Fillets, cutlets, steaks	450g (1lb)	4–5 min	Cook covered; stand 5–10 min
Whole fish	900g (2lb)	10–12 min	Slit skin 3 times on each side; cook covered; turn over during cooking; stand 10 min
Trout	2×200g (7oz) 4×200g (7oz)	6–8 min 10–12 min	Slit skin 3 times on each side; cook covered; stand 5 min
Kippers	225g (8oz) 450g (1lb)	3 min 4½–5 min	Cook covered; stand 5 min
'Boil-in-the-bag' frozen kipper fillets	200g (7oz)	6 min	Slit top of bag and place on non-metallic plate; stand 2 min
'Boil-in-the-bag' fish in sauce	170g (6oz)	cook on LOW 6 min; stand 2 min; cook LOW for a further 5 min	Pierce hole in top of bag and place on non-metallic plate

Soused herrings *(serves 4)*

4 medium herrings, filleted
salt and freshly ground black pepper
1 medium onion, peeled and thinly sliced
6 peppercorns
2 bayleaves
150ml (¼pt) cider vinegar
150ml (¼pt) water

1 Place the fillets on a work surface, skin side down. Sprinkle the flesh with salt and pepper.
2 Roll up from head to tail and secure with wooden cocktail sticks.
3 Arrange in a single layer in a shallow oven-proof dish.
4 Add the onion, peppercorns and bayleaves. Mix the vinegar with the water and pour over the herrings.
5 Cover with plastic wrap and cook on HIGH for 4 min.
6 Rearrange the herrings in the dish. Re-cover and continue cooking on HIGH for a further 3 min or until the herrings are cooked.
7 Leave to cool in the cooking liquid. Refrigerate.
8 Remove cocktail sticks before serving with salad.

Note: *If preferred, the tails can be left on, and when the rolled fish are placed in the dish arrange them with the tails pointing upwards.*

VARIATION
Substitute small mackerel for herring, and proceed as given above.

Baked trout *(serves 4)*

4 trout, cleaned, heads and tails left on, each
    weighing 150–225g (6–8oz)
25g (1oz) butter, optional
grated lemon rind
lemon wedges
watercress
4 slices of stuffed olive

1 Wipe and dry the trout, inside and out, with kitchen paper.
2 Slit the skin diagonally three times on each side.
3 Place the butter, if used, in a shallow oven-proof dish which will accommodate the trout in a single layer.
4 Microwave on HIGH for 45 sec or until melted.
5 Coat the trout in the melted butter and arrange in the dish.
6 Protect the tails and eyes by covering with small pieces of smooth foil. Foil must not touch any part of the oven interior.
7 Cover with plastic wrap and microwave on HIGH for 6 min.
8 Rearrange the fish in the dish, re-cover and continue cooking on HIGH for a further 4–6 min, depending on the weight of fish used. Test for readiness after 4 min.
9 Leave to stand, covered, for 5 min.
10 Remove pieces of foil. Serve fish sprinkled with grated lemon rind, garnished with lemon wedges and watercress. Cover the eyes with sliced stuffed olive.

VARIATION

Baked stuffed trout: mix together 75g (3oz) brown breadcrumbs, 100g (4oz) peeled prawns or shrimps, 1tbsp lemon juice, salt and pepper. Bind the mixture together with beaten egg and divide it among 4 trout after step 2 above. Proceed to cook and serve as above.

Note: *2 trout will require a total cooking time of 6–8 min on* HIGH. *Actual time will depend on weight of fish. Proceed as above, rearranging the fish after 3 min.*

Scampi provençale *(serves 6)*

25g (1oz) butter or margarine
1 medium onion, peeled and finely chopped
1 clove garlic, finely chopped
1×397g (14oz) can peeled tomatoes, drained
    and roughly chopped
4×15ml tbsp (4tbsp) dry white wine
salt and pepper
1×15ml tbsp (1tbsp) finely chopped parsley
450g (1lb) frozen unbreaded scampi or Dublin
    Bay prawns
a few fresh whole prawns in their shells,
    optional

1 Place the butter or margarine in an ovenproof casserole and microwave on HIGH for 45 sec or until melted.
2 Stir in the onion and garlic. Cover and cook on HIGH for 3 min.
3 Add the tomatoes, wine, seasoning and parsley. Cover and microwave on HIGH for 4 min.
4 Add the frozen scampi or prawns; stir, cover and cook on HIGH for 3 min.
5 Stir well, separating the scampi or prawns if necessary.
6 Re-cover and continue cooking on HIGH for a further 2 min or until just heated through. Do not overheat.
7 Serve with crusty bread or boiled long-grain rice, garnished if liked with a few fresh whole prawns in their shells.

Note: *If using defrosted scampi or prawns, proceed as above to step 3. Add the drained scampi or prawns, stir, cover and cook on* HIGH *for 3 min or until just heated through. Do not overheat otherwise the fish will be overcooked and tough. Serve as suggested above.*

Scampi provençale (above); Fillets of sole duglère (page 44)

Fillets of sole duglère *(serves 4)*

2 sole, filleted
2 × 15ml tbsp (2tbsp) finely chopped onion
½ bayleaf
few sprigs of parsley
salt and pepper
150ml (¼pt) dry white wine
150ml (¼pt) water
25g (1oz) margarine
40g (1½oz) plain flour
3 × 15ml tbsp (3tbsp) single cream
2 medium tomatoes, skinned, de-seeded and diced
2 × 5ml tsp (2tsp) chopped parsley

1 Rinse and dry the fish.
2 Remove the dark skin and arrange the fillets in an ovenproof dish with the thickest parts towards the outside.
3 Add the onion, bayleaf, parsley, seasoning, white wine and water.
4 Cover and cook on HIGH for 5 min.
5 Remove bayleaf and parsley. Drain the fish, reserving the liquor, and keep warm, covered.
6 Place the margarine in an ovenproof jug and melt on HIGH for 1 min. Stir in the flour.
7 Gradually blend in the cooking liquor and whisk until smooth.
8 Cook on HIGH for 3–4 min until the sauce has thickened, stirring every minute.
9 Stir in the cream, tomatoes and chopped parsley.
10 Season to taste and pour the sauce over the fish.
11 If necessary, reheat on HIGH for 2 min before serving.

VARIATION

Sole véronique: at step 9 above, omit tomatoes and parsley. Stir in 75g (3oz) seedless green grapes after the cream. Proceed as steps 10 and 11 above, garnishing with a further 25g (1oz) seedless green grapes immediately before serving.

Sole bonne femme *(serves 6)*

900g (2lb) sole fillets
1 small onion, peeled and finely chopped
100g (4oz) small button mushrooms
salt and pepper
4 × 15ml tbsp (4tbsp) dry white wine
1 bayleaf
40g (1½oz) margarine
40g (1½oz) plain flour
milk
3 × 15ml tbsp (3tbsp) cream
chopped chives, optional

1 Fold each fillet in three.
2 Remove stems from mushrooms and retain caps.
3 Place the onion, chopped mushroom stems and seasoning in a shallow ovenproof dish.
4 Lay the fish on top and pour over the wine. Add bayleaf.
5 Cover with plastic wrap and microwave on HIGH for 8 min or until fish flakes easily. Rearrange fish after 4 min.
6 Strain and reserve the cooking liquor, remove bayleaf and keep fish warm.
7 Place the mushroom caps in a small ovenproof bowl, cover and cook on HIGH for 1½ min. Leave to stand, covered.
8 Place the margarine in an ovenproof jug and melt on HIGH for about 1 min.
9 Blend in the flour, then gradually blend in the reserved cooking liquid made up to 300ml (½pt) with milk.
10 Microwave on HIGH for 3½–4 min until sauce has boiled and thickened. Stir after every minute.
11 Stir in the cream and pour the sauce over the fish.
12 Garnish with the drained cooked mushroom caps and, if necessary, reheat on HIGH for about 2 min before serving.
13 Sprinkle with chopped chives, if used.

Browning dish fish fingers (serves 3)

1 pack of 10 commercially frozen fish fingers
vegetable oil
2 medium tomatoes, sliced, optional
chopped parsley

1 Brush the fish fingers on both sides with oil.
2 Preheat a microwave browning dish according to manufacturer's instructions.
3 Place the frozen fish fingers carefully onto the hot surface, pressing them down well.
4 Microwave on HIGH for about 2 min until browned underneath.
5 Turn the fish fingers over, add the tomato slices, if used, and microwave on HIGH for about 3 min until cooked.
6 Serve sprinkled with parsley, accompanied by oven chips and tartare sauce.

Note: *The actual time taken to brown and cook the fish fingers will depend on starting temperature.*

VARIATIONS
Frozen fish cakes (1 pack of 4): proceed as above to step 3. Microwave on HIGH for 2 min or until browned underneath. Turn over, add tomato slices if used, and microwave on HIGH for $2\frac{1}{2}$ min or until cooked (see note above).
Frozen fish portions in batter (1 pack of 2): there is no need to brush battered foods with oil. Preheat microwave browning dish according to manufacturer's instructions. Place the battered fish portions onto the hot surface, press down well, and cook on HIGH for $2\frac{1}{2}$ min. Turn over and cook on HIGH for about a further $2\frac{1}{2}$ min or until cooked.

Kippers (serves 3)

450g (1lb) kippers, whole or filleted

1 Place the fish in a shallow ovenproof dish, overlapping the thinner edges of the fish.
2 Cover with plastic wrap and microwave on HIGH for $4\frac{1}{2}$ min or until flesh flakes easily when tested with a fork. Do not overcook.
3 Leave to stand, covered, for 2 min before serving.

Note: *To cook 1 whole kipper, place it on an ovenproof plate, without metal trim, and cover with plastic wrap. Microwave on HIGH for $1\frac{1}{2}$–2 min, depending on size. Leave to stand, covered, for 2 min before serving.*

Poached Haddock (serves 3)

450g (1lb) smoked haddock
4×15ml tbsp (4tbsp) milk

1 Arrange the fish in a single layer in a shallow ovenproof dish. Pour the milk over the fish.
2 Cover with plastic wrap and microwave on HIGH for $4\frac{1}{2}$–5 min until flesh flakes easily when tested with a fork. Test at $4\frac{1}{2}$ min. Do not overcook.
3 Leave to stand, covered, for 2 min.
4 Either serve fish on its own with crusty bread, or topped with a baked or poached egg.

Paupiettes of plaice (serves 4)

4×170g (6oz) fillets of plaice, skinned
salt and pepper
lemon juice
25g (1oz) margarine
25g (1oz) plain flour
300ml ($\frac{1}{2}$pt) milk, approximately
chopped parsley

1 Cut the fillets in half lengthways; season with salt, pepper and lemon juice.
2 Roll up from tail to head and arrange in a 1 litre ($1\frac{3}{4}$pt) ovenproof dish.
3 Cover with plastic wrap and microwave on HIGH for 6–7 min. Leave to stand, covered, and keep warm.
4 Place the margarine in an ovenproof jug and melt on HIGH for 1 min.
5 Stir in the flour, then blend in the strained cooking liquor from the fish made up to 300ml ($\frac{1}{2}$pt) with milk.
6 Microwave on HIGH for 3–4 min until the sauce thickens, stirring every minute. Season to taste.
7 Pour the sauce over the fish and sprinkle with chopped parsley before serving.

Cheesy fish pie (serves 4)

450g (1lb) white fish fillets
675g (1½lb) potatoes, peeled and cut into
  even-sized pieces
4×15ml tbsp (4tbsp) water
4×15ml tbsp (4tbsp) milk
25g (1oz) butter
salt and pepper
25g (1oz) margarine
25g (1oz) plain flour
milk
50g (2oz) grated cheese
2×15ml tbsp (2tbsp) grated cheese
chopped parsley

1 Arrange the fish on an ovenproof plate or in an ovenproof dish, with the thicker parts towards the outside.
2 Cover with plastic wrap and microwave on HIGH for 5 min. Leave to stand, covered.
3 Place potatoes in an ovenproof dish with the water. Cover with plastic wrap and microwave on HIGH for 12 min, stirring or shaking after 6 min.
4 Mash the potatoes with the milk and butter and beat until creamy. Season and leave to stand, covered.
5 Place the margarine in an ovenproof jug and microwave on HIGH for 1 min or until melted.
6 Stir in the flour, then blend in the strained cooking liquor from the fish made up to 300ml (½pt) with milk.
7 Microwave on HIGH for 3–4 min until sauce thickens, stirring every minute.
8 Season sauce and stir in 50g (2oz) grated cheese.
9 Flake the fish and stir into the sauce.
10 Place the fish mixture in a 1.1 litre (2pt) ovenproof pie dish and cover with the creamed potatoes.
11 Microwave on HIGH for 3 min.
12 Sprinkle with the 2tbsp grated cheese and brown under a preheated conventional grill.
13 Sprinkle with chopped parsley before serving.

Tuna crisp (serves 4–6)

1×295g (10½oz) can condensed cream of
  mushroom or cream of chicken soup,
  undiluted
2×200g (7oz) cans tuna fish, drained and flaked
2–3 medium tomatoes, sliced
1 small packet potato crisps, crushed
75g (3oz) grated cheese

1 Turn the soup into an ovenproof jug and microwave on HIGH for 3 min, stirring after 1½ min.
2 Place the fish in the bottom of a shallow ovenproof dish.
3 Cover with sliced tomato and pour soup over.
4 Mix the crushed crisps with the cheese and sprinkle on top.
5 Microwave on HIGH for 3 min or until heated through to the centre and cheese has melted.
6 Brown under a preheated conventional grill, if preferred.

Stuffed cod steaks (serves 4)

1 medium onion, peeled and finely chopped
2×15ml tbsp (2tbsp) water
2×5ml tsp (2tsp) mixed dried herbs
50g (2oz) brown or white breadcrumbs
1×15ml tbsp (1tbsp) lemon juice
salt and pepper
4×150g (6oz) cod steaks
25g (1oz) butter, flaked

1 Place the onion and water in an ovenproof bowl. Cover and microwave on HIGH for 2 min.
2 Stir in the mixed herbs, breadcrumbs, lemon juice and seasoning.
3 Stuff the cod steaks with the mixture and arrange them in a single layer in an ovenproof casserole.
4 Dot with flaked butter, cover the casserole and microwave on HIGH for about 7 min or until the fish flakes when tested with a fork.
5 Leave to stand, covered, for 2–3 min before serving.

Beef and tomato casserole (page 53); Lyonnaise potatoes (page 72); Petits pois

Meat and poultry

Frozen meat and poultry must be completely defrosted before cooking. The end results will largely depend on the quality of the raw meat and poultry, and it is best to use prime quality cuts to avoid disappointment. Since Yorkshire pudding and roast potatoes must be cooked in a conventional oven, it makes sense to roast beef this way too, leaving the microwave oven free to cook the vegetables, sauces and desserts.

Evenly shaped joints of meat and well-trussed poultry will cook best and require less attention. The narrow end of a leg of lamb and the wing tips and bone ends of poultry should be shielded with smooth pieces of aluminium foil for half the cooking time, if the oven manufacturer allows. Joints of meat and whole poultry should be turned over during defrosting and cooking. Use wooden skewers or cocktail sticks to secure meat in position or to truss poultry. Replace metal ties on pierced roasting bags with string or elastic bands. Joints of meat and poultry should be raised out of their cooking juices by placing them on a microwave roasting rack or upturned saucer or plate without metal trim. Pour off juices during cooking, since these absorb microwave energy and slow down cooking.

Use a meat thermometer to determine the readiness of meat and poultry, but remember that only special microwave thermometers can be placed in the oven. Ordinary meat thermometers can of course be used outside the oven.

Cook meat casseroles the day before they are required, cool and refrigerate overnight, and reheat gently the following day, stirring during reheating. This helps to tenderise the meat and allows time for flavours to mature. Joints of meat and whole poultry can be browned and crisped by placing under a preheated conventional grill or in a conventional oven at the end of the microwave cooking period. A microwave browning dish is useful for cooking steaks, chops, sausages and burgers.

Allow meat and poultry dishes to stand after cooking before serving. Joints of meat and whole poultry are covered with foil, shiny side in, during this standing time to allow the internal temperature to rise before serving.

Guide to defrosting meat and poultry

Food	Quantity	Approximate Time on LOW Setting	Special Instructions
Beef			
joints	per 450g (1lb)	8–10 min	Turn over during defrosting; stand for 1 hr
mince	per 450g (1lb)	7–10 min	Break up during defrosting; stand 10 min
steak, cubed	per 450g (1lb)	7–10 min	Separate during defrosting; stand 10 min

Food	Quantity	Approximate Time on LOW Setting	Special Instructions
Lamb/Veal			
joints	per 450g (1lb)	6–8 min	Turn over during defrosting; stand for 1 hr
liver, kidney	per 450g (1lb)	8–10 min	Separate during defrosting; stand 10 min
chops	2×100g (4oz)	4–5 min	Separate during defrosting; stand 5 min
Pork			
joints	per 450g (1lb)	8–10 min	Turn over during defrosting; stand for 1 hr
chops	2×225g (8oz)	6–8 min	Separate during defrosting; stand 10 min
Sausages	450g (1lb)	6–7 min	Separate during defrosting; stand 10 min
Bacon			
joints	per 450g (1lb)	6–8 min	Slit vacuum pack; turn joint over during defrosting; stand 20 min
rashers	225g (8oz)	2–3 min	Turn pack over during defrosting; stand 5 min
steaks	2×100g (4oz)	3–5 min	Separate during defrosting; stand 5 min
POULTRY **Chicken**			
whole	per 450g (1lb)	6–8 min	Turn over during defrosting; stand in cold water 30 min; remove giblets
portions	2×225g (8oz)	7–9 min	Turn over during defrosting; stand 10 min
Duckling	per 450g (1lb)	6–8 min	Turn over during defrosting; stand in cold water 20 min; remove giblets

Guide to cooking meat and poultry

Food	Quantity	Approximate time on HIGH Setting	Special instructions
Beef			
joints	per 450g (1lb)	rare 5–6 min medium 6–7 min well done 8–9 min	Turn over during cooking; stand 15–20 min, covered with foil
mince	450g (1lb)	5–6 min	Cook covered; stir during cooking; stand 3 min

Food	Quantity	Approximate time on HIGH Setting	Special instructions
Lamb/Veal			
joints	per 450g (1lb)	9–10 min	Turn over during cooking; stand 15–20 min, covered with foil
liver, kidney	450g (1lb)	6–8 min	Cook covered; rearrange during cooking; stand 5 min
chops	2×100g (4oz)	5–6 min	Turn over during cooking; best cooked in microwave browning dish
Pork			
joints	per 450g (1lb)	9–10 min	Turn over during cooking; stand 15–20 min, covered with foil
chops	2×225g (8oz)	10–11 min	Turn over during cooking; best cooked in microwave browning dish
Bacon joints	per 450g (1lb)	10 min	Turn over during cooking; stand 15 min, covered with foil
POULTRY Chicken			
whole	per 450g (1lb)	6–8 min	Turn over during cooking; stand 10–15 min, covered with foil
portions	2×225g (8oz)	8–10 min	Cook covered; turn over during cooking; stand 5 min
Duckling	per 450g (1lb)	6–8 min	Turn over during cooking; stand 10–15 min, covered with foil
Turkey			
unstuffed	per 450g (1lb)	8–9 min	Turn over 3–4 times during cooking; stand 15 min, covered with foil
stuffed	per 450g (1lb)	9–10 min	

Roast leg of lamb (serves 4–6)

leg of lamb weighing about 1.8kg (4lb)
microwave browning mix

1 Shield the narrow end of the joint by wrapping in a small piece of smooth foil. Do not allow the foil to touch any part of the oven interior.
2 Place the joint on a microwave roasting rack, or on an upturned plate or saucer without metal trim, in a dish to catch the juices.
3 Sprinkle with microwave browning mix and place in the oven.
4 Microwave on HIGH for 20 min.
5 Pour off excess meat juices, remove the foil from the narrow end and turn the joint over.
6 Sprinkle with microwave browning mix and continue cooking on HIGH for a further 20 min or until a meat thermometer inserted into the thickest part of the joint, avoiding the bone, registers 82°C (180°F). Juices should be clear.
7 Remove from the oven and cover the joint with a tent of foil, shiny side in, and leave to stand for 15–20 min before serving.

Note: The times given above are for lamb, well done. If meat is preferred less well done, cook for 18 min at step 4. Proceed as above and cook for a further 18 min on HIGH or until a meat thermometer registers 80°C (175°F). Cover and leave to stand as above.

Roast leg of lamb (above); Vichy carrots (pages 76–7)

Shepherd's pie *(serves 4–5)*

1 medium onion, peeled and finely chopped
150ml ($\frac{1}{4}$pt) boiling lamb stock or gravy
Approx. 450g (1lb) left-over cooked lamb, minced
2×5ml tsp (2tsp) Worcestershire sauce
1×15ml tbsp (1tbsp) tomato purée
salt and pepper
450g (1lb) left-over cooked mashed potato
paprika, optional

1 Place the onion with a tablespoon of water in a flameproof casserole or pie dish.
2 Cover and microwave on HIGH for 3 min.
3 Stir in stock or gravy, minced lamb, Worcestershire sauce and tomato purée. Season to taste.
4 Spread or pipe potato on top.
5 Microwave on HIGH for 5 min or until heated through.
6 Sprinkle with paprika, or brown top under a preheated conventional grill before serving.

Beef olives *(serves 4)*

Stuffing
1 small onion, peeled and finely chopped
50g (2oz) margarine
75g (3oz) breadcrumbs
25g (1oz) grated Parmesan cheese
1×15ml tbsp (1tbsp) chopped parsley
salt and pepper
beaten egg to bind

4 thinly cut slices rump or sirloin steak, each weighing about 100g (4oz)
1×397g (14oz) can tomatoes
1 bayleaf
4×15ml tbsp (4tbsp) red wine
salt and pepper
chopped parsley to garnish

1 To prepare stuffing: place onion and margarine in a Pyrex or ovenproof bowl. Cover and microwave on HIGH for 2 min.
2 Stir in remaining stuffing ingredients, binding together with beaten egg.
3 Beat the slices of meat until very thin and cut each slice in half.
4 Divide the stuffing between the meat slices.

5 Roll up and secure in position with wooden cocktail sticks.
6 Arrange in a single layer in a shallow ovenproof casserole.
7 Chop the tomatoes and add with their juice, to the casserole.
8 Add the bayleaf, wine and seasoning.
9 Cover the casserole with a tight-fitting lid or plastic wrap and microwave on HIGH for 6 min.
10 Turn the olives over, rearrange in the casserole, re-cover and continue cooking on HIGH for a further 4 min or until meat is tender.
11 Leave to stand, covered, for 5 min.
12 Remove bayleaf. Garnish with chopped parsley before serving.

Meatballs in tomato sauce *(serves 4)*

450g (1lb) lean minced beef
25g (1oz) fresh brown breadcrumbs
1 medium onion, peeled and finely chopped
$\frac{1}{2}$×5ml tsp ($\frac{1}{2}$tsp) garlic powder
1×15ml tbsp (1tbsp) finely chopped parsley
salt and pepper
beaten egg to bind
1×298g (10$\frac{1}{2}$oz) can condensed tomato and rice soup, undiluted
150ml (5fl oz) water

1 Mix together all the ingredients, except the soup and water.
2 Divide the meat mixture into 12 to 16 pieces and shape into balls.
3 Arrange the meatballs in a single layer in a shallow ovenproof dish, preferably in a ring in a 25cm (10in) round dish.
4 Microwave on HIGH for 5 min.
5 Drain off any fat, cover and set aside.
6 Meanwhile mix the soup and water together in an ovenproof jug. Cover and microwave on HIGH for 4 min. Stir after 2 min.
7 Turn the meatballs over and rearrange if they are not being cooked in a ring (bring meatballs from the outside of the dish to the centre and vice versa).
8 Pour the soup mixture over the meatballs and microwave on HIGH for 5 min or until the meatballs are fully cooked.

Beef and tomato casserole *(serves 6)*

675g (1½lb) braising steak
225g (8oz) prepared weight carrots, sliced
225g (8oz) prepared onion, chopped
1×425g (15oz) can tomato soup
100g (4oz) small button mushrooms
salt and pepper

1 Pierce the meat all over with a fork and cut into 2.5cm (1in) cubes.
2 Place in a large round ovenproof casserole. Cover with a tight-fitting lid or plastic wrap and microwave on HIGH for 6 min, stirring after 3 min to bring brown meat to the centre and pink meat to the outside of the casserole.
3 Drain off any fat.
4 Stir in remaining ingredients, re-cover and microwave on HIGH for 5 min or until stew is boiling.
5 Reduce setting to LOW and continue cooking for a further 45 min or until meat is tender.
6 Leave to stand, covered, for 10 min before serving.

Note: *The flavour of this casserole is even better if it is cooked the day before it is required. Cool and refrigerate. Next day reheat, covered, on* HIGH *for at least 5 min until just boiling. Stir after every 2 min.*

Chilli con carne *(serves 4–6)*

450g (1lb) lean minced beef
1 large onion, peeled and finely chopped
1×397g (14oz) can tomatoes
2×15ml tbsp (2tbsp) tomato purée
salt and pepper
2×5ml tsp (2tsp) chilli powder, or to taste
1×425g (15oz) can red kidney beans, drained

1 Place the minced beef in a large ovenproof casserole and break up with a fork.
2 Cover with a lid or plastic wrap and microwave on HIGH for 4 min.
3 Drain off any fat, break up the meat with a fork and stir in the chopped onion.
4 Re-cover and microwave on HIGH for a further 4 min or until the meat is no longer pink. Stir after 2 min.
5 Stir in the tomatoes with their juice, tomato purée, salt, pepper and chilli powder to taste.
6 Re-cover and cook on HIGH for 10 min, stirring during cooking.
7 Stir in the drained beans, reduce setting to LOW, re-cover and cook for a further 25 min. Stir occasionally during cooking.
8 Serve with rice or pasta.

Note: *The flavour of this dish is even better if it is cooked the day before it is required, allowed to cool and refrigerated. Next day reheat, covered, on* HIGH *for about 5 min or until just boiling. Stir after every 2 min.*

Roast beef *(serves 6–8)*

1×1.8kg (4lb) joint boned and rolled sirloin, preferably 10–12.5cm (4–5in) in diameter

1 Place the joint on an upturned plate or saucer without metal trim, or on a microwave roasting rack, in a dish to catch the juices.
2 Calculate the total cooking time, allowing 6 min per 450g (1lb) for rare, 7 min per 450g (1lb) for medium, and 9 min per 450g (1lb) for well-done beef.
3 Microwave on HIGH for half the total cooking time.
4 Pour off excess meat juices, turn joint over, and continue cooking on HIGH for remaining time, or until a meat thermometer inserted in the centre of the joint registers 55°C (130°F) rare, 65°C (150°F) medium, or 70°C (160°F) well done.
5 Wrap the joint in foil, shiny side in, and leave to stand for 15–20 min before serving.

Note: *The joint can be cooked in a roasting bag. Simply place the joint in the bag, pierce the bag in at least three places and fasten the end loosely with a piece of string or an elastic band. Place on an upturned plate or saucer, or on a microwave roasting rack in a dish, and proceed as above. Cooking in a roasting bag tends to encourage browning.*

Beef and vegetable cobbler *(serves 4–6)*

1 large onion, peeled and finely chopped
450g (1lb) minced beef
2×5ml tsp (2tsp) plain flour
2 medium carrots, peeled and finely diced
½ green pepper, de-seeded and diced
50g (2oz) mushrooms, sliced
1×5ml tsp (1tsp) dried mixed herbs
1×397g (14oz) can tomatoes
150ml (¼pt) boiling beef stock
1×15ml tbsp (1tbsp) tomato purée
salt and pepper
Topping
40g (1½oz) block margarine
150g (6oz) self-raising wholewheat flour
1×5ml tsp (1tsp) dried mixed herbs
pinch of salt
120ml (4fl oz) milk, approximately
½×5ml tsp (½tsp) beef and vegetable extract

1 Place the onion with a tablespoon of water in a 2 litre (3½pt) ovenproof round casserole. Cover and cook on HIGH for 4 min.
2 Stir in crumbled minced beef, cover and cook for 5 min, breaking down lumps of mince after 2½ min.
3 Drain off any fat and stir well.
4 Stir in remaining ingredients except topping; cover and microwave on HIGH for 15 min, stirring every 5 min.
5 Meanwhile make topping. Rub margarine into flour until mixture resembles fine breadcrumbs.
6 Stir in herbs and salt. Mix with enough milk to give a soft dough.
7 Knead dough lightly on a floured board, and roll out to 1.25cm (½in) thick.
8 Cut dough into eight 5cm (2in) rounds, and brush tops with the beef and vegetable extract which has been mixed with 1tsp boiling water.
9 Uncover the meat mixture and place the scones on top, around the outside of the casserole.
10 Microwave on HIGH for about 7 min until the scones are well risen and cooked.

Gourmet goulash *(serves 4–5)*

675g (1½lb) topside of beef, cut into 2.5cm (1in) cubes
30ml (1fl oz) vegetable oil
300ml (½pt) water
150ml (¼pt) dry red wine
1×42g (1½oz) packet seasoning mix for goulash
1 small green pepper, de-seeded and sliced
350g (12oz) ribbon noodles
3×15ml tbsp (3tbsp) soured cream or natural yoghurt
paprika

1 Place the meat and oil in a 2 litre (3½pt) ovenproof casserole.
2 Cover with a lid or plastic wrap and cook on HIGH for 6 min, stirring after 3 min to separate meat and bring brown meat to the centre and pink meat to the outside edges of the casserole.
3 Blend together the water, wine and seasoning mix.
4 Drain off any excess fat from the meat, stir in the blended seasoning mixture together with the green pepper.
5 Re-cover and cook on HIGH for 5 min or until boiling.
6 Reduce setting to LOW and continue cooking for about 40 min, stirring occasionally.
7 Test meat for tenderness and, if necessary, continue cooking on LOW for a further 10 min. Leave to stand, covered.
8 Meanwhile place the noodles with 900ml (1½pt) boiling water and 1tbsp vegetable oil in a large ovenproof casserole.
9 Stir, cover tightly with a lid or plastic wrap and cook on HIGH for 6 min or until *al dente* (tender but still firm).
10 Leave noodles to stand for 2–3 min before draining.
11 Stir the soured cream or yoghurt into the goulash, sprinkle with paprika and serve with the freshly cooked noodles.

Pollo cacciatore (page 57); Spicy sprouts (page 77); Party drumsticks (page 58)

Cottage pie *(serves 4–5)*

450g (1lb) prepared weight peeled potatoes
4×15ml tbsp (4tbsp) water
1 medium onion, peeled and finely chopped
450g (1lb) minced beef
2×5ml tsp (2tsp) plain flour
1×5ml tsp (1tsp) dried mixed herbs
salt and pepper
1×5ml tsp (1tsp) Worcestershire sauce
150ml (¼pt) hot beef stock
1×15ml tbsp (1tbsp) milk
25g (1oz) butter
paprika, optional

1 Cut the prepared potatoes into 25g (1oz) pieces and place with the water in an ovenproof bowl or casserole.
2 Microwave on HIGH for 10 min, stirring or shaking at least once during cooking. Leave to stand, covered.
3 Meanwhile place the onion with a tablespoon of water in a large flameproof casserole. Cover and microwave on HIGH for 2 min.
4 Stir the minced beef into the onion, cover and cook on HIGH for 3 min.
5 Break mince down with a fork, stir well, re-cover and continue cooking on HIGH for a further 3 min.
6 Stir in flour, herbs, seasoning, Worcestershire sauce and stock.
7 Cover and cook on HIGH for 5 min.
8 Drain the potatoes and mash with the milk and butter. Season.
9 Spread or pipe the mashed potato over the meat.
10 Microwave on HIGH for 2–3 min until heated through.
11 Brown the top of the pie under a preheated conventional grill or, alternatively sprinkle with paprika.

Beef and mushroom pudding *(serves 4–5)*

25g (1oz) margarine
1 large onion, peeled and chopped
100g (4oz) mushrooms, sliced
350g (12oz) lean minced beef
salt and pepper

Suet pastry
150g (6oz) self-raising flour
50g (2oz) breadcrumbs
100g (4oz) shredded suet
180ml (6fl oz) cold water to mix, approximately

1 Place the margarine, onion and mushrooms in an ovenproof bowl.
2 Cover and microwave on HIGH for 4 min, stirring after 2 min.
3 Stir in minced beef and seasoning.
4 Re-cover and microwave on HIGH for 5 min, stirring after 2½ min. Drain off excess liquid.
5 To make the pastry, mix the dry ingredients with enough cold water to form a light elastic dough. Knead lightly.
6 Roll out two-thirds of the pastry and line a greased 1.1 litre (2pt) ovenproof pudding bowl.
7 Turn the meat mixture into the bowl.
8 Roll out remaining pastry to make a lid. Wet the edge with water and seal the pastry edges well together.
9 Cover loosely with greased greaseproof paper and microwave on HIGH for 9 min.
10 Leave to stand for 2 min before serving from the bowl, or carefully turning out onto a heated serving dish.

Upside down meat loaf *(serves 6)*

3×5ml tsp (3tsp) soft brown sugar
1×227g (8oz) can pineapple rings
350g (12oz) raw lean minced beef
350g (12oz) cooked ham, or cooked bacon joint, minced
75g (3oz) breadcrumbs
1 medium onion, peeled and minced
salt and pepper
½×5ml tsp (½tsp) dried mixed herbs
1 egg, beaten
scant 1×5ml tsp (1tsp) arrowroot

1 Sprinkle brown sugar over the base of a lightly greased 22.5×12.5cm (9×5in) microwave loaf dish.
2 Drain the pineapple, reserving the juice, and arrange the slices over the sugar in the base of the dish.
3 Mix together remaining ingredients, except

the arrowroot, and press firmly and evenly into the dish.

4 Cover loosely with greaseproof paper and microwave on HIGH for 5 min.

5 Pour off juices, re-cover with greaseproof paper and microwave on LOW for 18–20 min until a meat thermometer inserted in the centre of the loaf registers 75°C (170°F).

6 Cover with foil, shiny side in, and leave to stand.

7 Meanwhile pour reserved pineapple juice into a Pyrex measuring jug and make up to 150ml ($\frac{1}{4}$pt) with water.

8 Blend arrowroot with a little of the measured liquid, then stir into remaining liquid until smooth.

9 Microwave on HIGH for 2 min or until thickened.

10 Turn the meat loaf onto a serving plate so that pineapple slices are on top, and pour the sauce over.

11 Serve hot or cold.

Minced beef ring *(serves 4)*

450g (1lb) minced beef
4 × 15ml tbsp (4tbsp) rolled oats
1 medium onion, peeled and finely chopped
$\frac{1}{2}$ × 5ml tsp ($\frac{1}{2}$tsp) dried mixed herbs
salt and pepper
1 egg, beaten
4 × 15ml tbsp (4tbsp) tomato sauce
1 × 15ml tbsp (1tbsp) soft brown sugar
dash of Worcestershire sauce

1 Mix together the minced beef, oats, onion, herbs and seasoning. Bind mixture together with beaten egg.

2 Place a glass jar or tumbler (not lead crystal) in the centre of a 22.5cm (9in) pie plate or dish.

3 Shape the meat mixture around the jar or tumbler.

4 Cover loosely with greaseproof paper and microwave on HIGH for 5 min. Pour off meat juices.

5 Mix the tomato sauce with the sugar and Worcestershire sauce and spoon or brush over the meat ring, coating the top and sides.

6 Re-cover with greaseproof paper and cook on LOW for 9 min or until a meat thermometer inserted in the meat ring registers 75°C (170°F).

7 Cover with foil, shiny side in, and stand for at least 5 min before serving.

VARIATION

Substitute tomato ketchup or barbecue sauce for the tomato sauce, sugar and Worcestershire sauce mixture.

Pollo cacciatore *(serves 4)*

25g (1oz) butter or margarine
1 medium onion, sliced and separated into rings
1 clove garlic, minced or finely chopped
$\frac{1}{2}$ × 5ml tsp ($\frac{1}{2}$tsp) dried oregano
4 chicken portions
1 × 397g (14oz) can tomatoes
salt and pepper
1 × 15ml tbsp (1tbsp) chopped parsley
3 × 15ml tbsp (3tbsp) dry white wine, optional
chopped parsley to garnish

1 Place the butter or margarine, onion, garlic and oregano in an ovenproof casserole.

2 Cover and microwave on HIGH for 3 min.

3 Add the chicken portions, skinned if preferred, and coat in the mixture. Arrange portions with meatiest parts towards outside of dish.

4 Purée the contents of the can or tomatoes in an electric blender or food processor. Stir in the salt, pepper, chopped parsley and wine, if used.

5 Pour or spoon the purée over the chicken to coat it completely.

6 Cover and microwave on HIGH for 12 min.

7 Turn chicken portions over, coat with sauce and re-cover.

8 Continue cooking on HIGH for a further 12–14 min, depending on size of portions.

9 Leave to stand, covered, for 5 min.

10 Sprinkle with chopped parsley before serving.

Party drumsticks *(makes 8)*

8 chicken drumsticks, each weighing about
    100g (4oz)
microwave seasoning for chicken, or seasoned
    crumb mix for chicken
parsley sprigs

1 Skin the drumsticks, if preferred. Sprinkle with microwave seasoning or coat in seasoned crumb mix.
2 Arrange the drumsticks, preferably on a microwave roasting rack, in an ovenproof dish with the thin bony ends towards the centre.
3 Microwave on HIGH for 8 min.
4 Pour off juices, turn drumsticks over, and continue cooking on HIGH for a further 9 min or until juices run clear and chicken is tender. Check for readiness towards the end of the cooking period, removing any drumsticks which are cooked.
5 Leave to stand for a few minutes before serving, or leave till cold. Garnish with parsley sprigs.

VARIATION
Coated chicken thighs: substitute 8 × 100g (4oz) chicken thighs for drumsticks and proceed as above.

Roast chicken *(serves 5–6)*

1 × 1.8kg (4lb) chicken, at room temperature,
    giblets removed
microwave seasoning for chicken, optional

1 Remove giblets. Wash the chicken inside and outside, and dry thoroughly with kitchen paper.
2 Truss well, so that the legs and wings are held close to the body, to give a compact shape.
3 Wrap small pieces of smooth foil around the wing tips and leg ends to shield them.
4 Sprinkle the chicken with the seasoning, if used, and place in a roasting bag.
5 Pierce the bag in at least three places and fasten the end loosely with string or an elastic band.

6 Place the chicken, breast side down, on an upturned plate or saucer without metal trim, or on a microwave roasting rack, in a dish to catch the juices.
7 Microwave on HIGH for 12 min.
8 Drain off excess juices, remove pieces of foil, and turn chicken over, breast side up.
9 Continue cooking on HIGH for a further 12 min or until a meat thermometer inserted in the thickest part of each thigh registers at least 85°C (185°F). Juices should run clear.
10 Remove from oven and cover with a tent of foil, shiny side in, and leave to stand for 10–15 min. During this time the temperature in the thickest part of each thigh should rise to 90°C (195°F).
11 Remove the chicken from the roasting bag and serve hot or cold.
12 If preferred, breast may be browned and crisped under a preheated conventional grill.

Note:
1 *The chicken can be cooked without a roasting bag. Proceed as above, but at steps 7 and 9 cook on* HIGH *for about 14 min. Chicken may be browned under a preheated conventional grill before serving, if preferred.*
2 *If chicken is stuffed, allow an extra minute per 450g (1lb).*

VARIATION
Roast turkey: follow manufacturer's recommendations regarding the size of turkey which can be cooked satisfactorily in your oven. Prepare and proceed as for Roast Chicken, with or without a roasting bag, allowing 8–9 min per 450g (1lb) and turning the turkey over three or four times during cooking, depending on size. If stuffed, allow 9–10 min per 450g (1lb). Test for readiness as for chicken, and leave to stand for 30 min before serving.

Roast chicken (above); Bacon rolls (page 121); Speedy 'roast' potatoes (page 70); Cranberry sauce (page 80); Sweetcorn

Chicken curry (serves 4)

25g (1oz) butter or margarine
1 medium onion, peeled and chopped
1–2×15ml tbsp (1–2tbsp) curry powder,
   according to taste
1×15ml tbsp (1tbsp) plain flour
600ml (1pt) chicken stock
1×5ml tsp (1tsp) Worcestershire sauce
2×5ml tsp (2tsp) tomato purée
2×5ml tsp (2tsp) lemon juice
2×15ml tbsp (2tbsp) mango chutney
1 dessert apple, peeled, cored and chopped
50g (2oz) sultanas
350g (12oz) cooked chicken meat, diced
salt and pepper
50g (2oz) salted peanuts

1 Place the butter or margarine with the onion
   in an ovenproof casserole. Cover and microwave on HIGH for 3 min.
2 Stir in the curry powder and flour and gradually blend in the stock.
3 Re-cover and microwave on HIGH for 5 min
   or until sauce has boiled and thickened. Stir
   every minute.
4 Stir in the Worcestershire sauce, tomato
   purée, lemon juice, chutney, apple and sultanas.
5 Cover and microwave on HIGH for 4 min.
6 Stir in the chicken, salt and pepper, and re-
   cover.
7 Microwave on HIGH for 3 min or until piping
   hot. Stir.
8 Leave to stand, covered, for 5 min before
   serving sprinkled with salted peanuts.
9 Serve with boiled long-grain rice, accompanied by sliced bananas, sliced tomatoes,
   chutney and desiccated coconut.

Note: *The flavour of a curry improves if it is
cooked the day before it is required. Cool and
refrigerate. Next day reheat, covered, on HIGH
for 5 min or until just boiling. Stir after every
2 min.*

VARIATION
Substitute cooked turkey meat or beef for
chicken and proceed as above.

Barbecue-style chicken (serves 4)

50g (2oz) raisins
1 medium onion, peeled and finely chopped
25g (1oz) butter or margarine
3×15ml tbsp (3tbsp) golden syrup
3×15ml tbsp (3tbsp) fruity brown sauce
3×15ml tbsp (3tbsp) tomato ketchup
dash of Worcestershire sauce
salt and pepper
pinch of mustard powder
4 chicken quarters, each weighing 280g–350g
   (10oz–12oz)

1 To plump the raisins, place them in a small
   ovenproof bowl. Barely cover them with
   water, cover the bowl with plastic wrap, and
   microwave on HIGH for 3 min. Stir and leave
   to stand for 5 min. Drain.
2 Place the onion with the butter or margarine
   in a large ovenproof casserole. Cover and
   microwave on HIGH for 3 min or until onion is
   tender.
3 Mix together the syrup, brown sauce, tomato
   ketchup, Worcestershire sauce, salt, pepper
   and mustard in an ovenproof jug.
4 Microwave on HIGH for 2 min, stirring after
   1 min. Stir in raisins.
5 Arrange the chicken quarters on top of the
   onion in the casserole, skin side down, and
   with the thickest parts towards the outside of
   the dish.
6 Pour the sauce over the chicken, cover with a
   tight-fitting lid or plastic wrap, and microwave on HIGH for 8 min.
7 Turn the chicken quarters over, skin side up,
   baste with sauce and re-cover.
8 Microwave on HIGH for a further 12 min or
   until chicken is tender.
9 Leave to stand, covered, for 10 min before
   serving.

Chicken à la king (serves 4)

50g (2oz) butter or margarine
2×15ml tbsp (2tbsp) chopped green pepper
2×15ml tbsp (2tbsp) chopped red pepper
100g (4oz) mushrooms, sliced
40g (1½oz) plain flour
150ml (¼pt) milk

300ml (½pt) chicken stock
350g (12oz) cooked chicken, roughly chopped
salt and pepper
pinch of ground nutmeg
2 × 15ml tbsp (2tbsp) sherry, optional
1 × 15ml tbsp (1tbsp) single cream, optional
parsley sprigs to garnish

1 Place the butter or margarine in a deep oven-proof casserole and microwave on HIGH for 1¼ min or until melted.
2 Stir in the peppers and mushrooms. Cover and cook on HIGH for 2 min, stirring after 1 min.
3 Stir in the flour and gradually blend in the milk and stock.
4 Microwave on HIGH for 5½ min or until just boiling, stirring after every minute.
5 Stir in the chicken, salt, pepper, nutmeg and sherry, if used.
6 Cover and cook on HIGH for about 4 min or until piping hot, stirring after 2 min.
7 Leave to stand, covered for 2 min. Stir in cream, if used. Garnish with parsley.
8 Serve on toasted crusty bread. Alternatively serve with buttered noodles, or as a light meal with crisp rolls.

VARIATION
Substitute left-over turkey for chicken.

Roast duckling (serves 4)

1 × 1.8kg (4lb) duckling
2 × 15ml tbsp (2tbsp) sieved plum jam
orange twists or slices and watercress, to garnish

1 Remove giblets. Wash the duckling inside and outside, and dry thoroughly with kitchen paper.
2 Truss firmly, so that the legs and wings are held close to the body, to give a compact shape.
3 Prick the skin all over to release fat during cooking.
4 Place the duckling, breast side down, on a microwave roasting rack or upturned saucer without metal trim, in an ovenproof

dish to catch the fat and juices. Brush with jam.
5 Wrap small pieces of smooth foil around the wing tips and leg ends to shield them.
6 Microwave on HIGH for 14 min. Remove foil pieces.
7 Pour off fat and turn duckling breast side up. Brush with jam.
8 Microwave on HIGH for about a further 14 min or until a meat thermometer inserted in the thickest part of each thigh registers 85°C (185°F) and juices run clear. Pour off fat during cooking if necessary.
9 Remove from oven and cover with a tent of foil, shiny side in, and leave to stand for 10–15 min.
10 Serve garnished with orange twists or slices and watercress, accompanied by an orange and cress salad plus vegetables of choice.

Tropical turkey (serves 2)

1 fresh pineapple
25g (1oz) butter or margarine
1 medium onion, peeled and finely chopped
2 × 15ml tbsp (2tbsp) chopped green pepper
2 × 15ml tbsp (2tbsp) chopped red pepper
100g (4oz) mushrooms, sliced
150–225g (6–8oz) cooked turkey meat, chopped
2 × 15ml tbsp (2tbsp) wine vinegar
2 × 5ml tsp (2tsp) demerara sugar
2 × 5ml tsp (2tsp) cornflour
180ml (6fl oz) turkey or chicken stock
dash of soy sauce
salt and pepper
paprika, optional

1 Cut the pineapple in half top to bottom and carefully remove the flesh. Reserve the shells and chop the flesh, removing the core.
2 Place the butter or margarine, onion and peppers in an ovenproof casserole. Cover and microwave on HIGH for 3 min, stirring after 1½ min.
3 Stir in the mushrooms, re-cover and cook for a further 2 min.
4 Stir in the chopped pineapple and turkey.
5 Blend the vinegar and sugar with the

cornflour in an ovenproof jug. Gradually stir in the stock.

6 Microwave on HIGH for 2½ min, stirring after every minute.
7 Stir into the casserole. Add the soy sauce and season to taste.
8 Cover the casserole and heat on HIGH for 4 min. Stir after 2 min.
9 Divide the mixture between the half pineapple shells.
10 Place the shells in an ovenproof dish, cover with plastic wrap and heat on HIGH for about 1 min to warm the shells.
11 Serve sprinkled with paprika, if liked, and accompanied by a side salad.

VARIATION

Tropical chicken: substitute cooked chicken meat for turkey and proceed as above.

Bacon joint *(serves 6)*

1 × 1.3kg (3lb) joint of unsmoked bacon

1 Soak the joint overnight in cold water if it is thought to be salty.
2 Drain well and pat dry with kitchen paper.
3 Place the joint in a roasting bag. Pierce the bag in at least three places and fasten the end loosely with string or an elastic band.
4 Place on an upturned plate or saucer, without metal trim, or on a microwave roasting rack, in a dish to catch the juices.
5 Microwave on HIGH for 15 min.
6 Turn joint over and pour off any excess juices from dish.
7 Reduce to LOW setting and continue cooking for a further 15 min or until the internal temperature reaches 80°C (175°F).
8 Remove from the oven and cover with a tent of foil, shiny side in, and leave to stand for 15 min before serving.

Note: *Cooked 'ready-to-eat' bacon joints are now available, and these only need reheating. Place in a roasting bag, as above, and heat on* LOW, *allowing about 20 min per 450g (1lb) or until internal temperature registers 55°C (130°F). Cover with foil and leave to stand as above before serving.*

Kidneys turbigo *(serves 4)*

12 baby onions, shallots or pickling onions
450g (1lb) lambs' kidneys
25g (1oz) butter or margarine
1 × 15ml tbsp (1tbsp) plain flour
1 × 5ml tsp (1tsp) tomato paste
100g (4oz) button mushrooms, halved
12 cocktail frankfurters, or 4 frankfurters each cut into three
3 × 15ml tbsp (3tbsp) sherry
120ml (4fl oz) brown stock
1 bayleaf
salt and pepper
4 slices bread, fried conventionally
chopped parsley

1 Peel the onions and fry them conventionally in a little oil until golden brown and cooked. Set aside.
2 Skin and halve the kidneys. Remove the cores with scissors.
3 Melt the butter or margarine in an ovenproof casserole on HIGH for 1 min.
4 Stir in the kidneys, cover with plastic wrap or a tight-fitting lid and microwave on HIGH for 6 min, stirring after 3 min.
5 Stir in the flour, tomato paste, mushrooms, frankfurters, onions, sherry and stock. Add the bayleaf and seasoning.
6 Re-cover and microwave on HIGH for a further 5 min or until the kidneys are tender. Stir after 2½ min. Do not overcook.
7 Leave the kidneys to stand, covered, for 5 min.
8 Meanwhile fry the bread conventionally in a little oil until golden brown. Drain well.
9 Remove the bayleaf from the casserole. Either spoon the kidneys over the fried bread, or cut the bread into small triangles and place around the outside edge of the casserole.
10 Sprinkle with chopped parsley before serving.

Tropical turkey (pages 61–2); Chicken and ham risotto (pages 88–9)

Gammon steaks (serves 4)

4 gammon steaks, each weighing 150–225g
(6–8oz)
watercress

1 Remove the rind from the gammon. Snip the fat at 1.25cm (½in) intervals to prevent curling during cooking.
2 Arrange the steaks in a single layer in an ovenproof shallow dish or on a large flat plate without metal trim.
3 Cover with kitchen paper and microwave on HIGH for 5 min.
4 Turn the steaks over, rearrange in the dish or on the plate.
5 Re-cover with kitchen paper and microwave on HIGH for a further 5 min.
6 Leave to stand, covered, for 2 min before serving garnished with watercress.

Note:

1 *If you wish to serve the steaks with pineapple, simply top each one with a pineapple ring for the final 2 min cooking time.*
2 *Gammon steaks tend to 'pop' during cooking.*

Braised pork chops (serves 2)

2×150g (6oz) trimmed weight pork chops, cut 1.25–2cm (½–¾in) thick
1½×15ml tbsp (1½tbsp) plain flour
1×5ml tsp (1tsp) mustard powder
1 small onion, peeled and finely chopped
2×15ml tbsp (2tbsp) chopped green pepper
1½×5ml tsp (1½tsp) gravy granules
1×397g (14oz) can tomatoes
2×5ml tsp (2tsp) Worcestershire sauce

1 Snip the outside edge of the chops and pierce both sides all over with a fork.
2 Mix the flour and mustard together and coat the chops with this mixture.
3 Place the chops in a single layer in an ovenproof casserole.
4 Top with the onion, pepper and gravy granules.
5 Chop the tomatoes roughly and mix with their juice and Worcestershire sauce.

6 Pour the tomato mixture over the chops.
7 Cover the casserole with a tight-fitting lid of plastic wrap and microwave on HIGH for 10 min.
8 Turn the chops over, spoon the vegetables and sauce over them and re-cover.
9 Microwave on HIGH for 5 min.
10 Reduce setting to LOW and continue cooking for a further 15 min or until chops are tender.

Liver, bacon and onions (serves 3–4)

4 rashers bacon, de-rinded
450g (1lb) calves' or lambs' liver, thinly sliced
2 medium onions, peeled and thinly sliced

1 Snip the bacon fat at regular intervals to prevent curling.
2 Place the bacon in a single layer in a shallow ovenproof dish.
3 Cover loosely with kitchen paper and microwave on HIGH for about 4 min. Remove bacon from the dish.
4 Coat the liver in the bacon fat and arrange with the onions in the dish.
5 Cover the dish with a tight-fitting lid or plastic wrap, and microwave on HIGH for 3 min.
6 Turn the liver over, re-cover and continue cooking on HIGH for a further 3 min or until liver is tender.
7 Lay the bacon rashers on top of the liver and onions, re-cover and microwave on HIGH for 1 min.
8 Leave to stand, covered, for 5 min before serving.

Vegetables

Vegetables cooked in a microwave oven retain their colour, are tender but crisp, and full of flavour. Very little water, usually only 4tbsp, is added to cook vegetables and some, such as mushrooms and spinach, do not require any water at all. Frozen vegetables also cook to perfection in a microwave oven.

It is really best to season vegetables after cooking, but if you prefer to add salt during cooking, add this to the water and do not sprinkle it on the vegetables, for this will cause dehydration and toughening.

Fresh vegetables can be blanched in a microwave oven – up to 450g (1lb) at a time. They should be cooked for half the time given in the chart and stirred during this time. After blanching, cool vegetables in iced water, before freezing.

Guide to cooking fresh vegetables

Prepare vegetables in the usual way. Place in a covered dish with 4tbsp of salted water, unless otherwise stated. Prick the skin of whole vegetables, ie potatoes, before cooking.

Vegetable	Quantity	Approximate Time on HIGH Setting	Special Instructions
Artichokes	4 medium	15–16 min	Rearrange during cooking; stand 2 min before serving
Asparagus spears	450g (1lb)	7–9 min	Arrange stalks towards outside of dish; stand 3 min before serving
Aubergines, sliced	450g (1lb)	8–10 min	Stir during cooking; stand 3 min before serving
Beans broad, shelled runner, sliced	 450g (1lb) 450g (1lb)	 8–9 min 10–12 min	Stir during cooking; stand 3 min before serving Stir during cooking; stand 2–3 min before serving
Beetroot peeled and sliced whole, medium	 450g (1lb) 4	 7–8 min 14–15 min	Shake during cooking; stand 3 min before serving Prick skin, wrap in plastic wrap; do not add water; skin after cooking
Broccoli spears	450g (1lb)	10–12 min	Place stalks towards outside of dish; rearrange during cooking

Vegetable	Quantity	Approximate Time on HIGH Setting	Special Instructions
Brussels sprouts	450g (1lb)	8–10 min	Cut a cross in stalk end; stir during cooking; stand 2–3 min before serving
Cabbage, shredded	450g (1lb)	9–10 min	Stir during cooking; stand 2–3 min before serving
Carrots, sliced	225g (8oz) 450g (1lb)	8–9 min 11–12 min	Stir during cooking; stand 3 min before serving
Cauliflower, florets	450g (1lb)	10–11 min	Stir during cooking; stand 2–3 min before serving
Celery, sliced	350g (12oz)	9–11 min	Stir during cooking; stand 3 min before serving
Corn-on-the-cob	2 cobs	6–8 min	Wrap individually in buttered greaseproof paper, no water; turn over during cooking
Courgettes, sliced	450g (1lb)	8–9 min	Do not add water; stir during cooking
Leeks, sliced	450g (1lb)	9–10 min	Stir or shake during cooking; stand 3 min before serving
Mushrooms	225g (8oz)	3–4 min	Do not add water; cook in 25g (1oz) butter; stir during cooking
Onions, sliced	225g (8oz)	5–7 min	Stir or shake during cooking
Parsnips, sliced	450g (1lb)	10–12 min	Stir during cooking; stand 3 min before serving
Peas	225g (8oz)	7–9 min	Stir during cooking; stand 2 min before serving
Potatoes jacket	2×225g (8oz)	9–10 min	Prick skin; place on kitchen paper; turn over during cooking; stand 5 min before serving
boiled	450g (1lb)	10 min	Cut into 25g (1oz) pieces; shake or stir during cooking; stand 3 min before serving
Spinach	450g (1lb)	6–7 min	Do not add water; stir during cooking
Swede/Turnip, diced	450g (1lb)	10–15 min	Stir during cooking, time will vary with age; stand 5 min drain and mash before serving

Ratatouille (page 69); Green beans amandine (page 69); Cauliflower cheese (page 69)

Guide to cooking frozen vegetables

Place the frozen vegetables with 4tbsp water, unless otherwise stated, in a non-metallic covered dish. Drain and season to taste.

Vegetable	Quantity	Approximate Time on HIGH Setting	Special Instructions
Asparagus spears	225g (8oz)	6–7 min	Separate spears during cooking; stand 2 min before serving
Beans			
broad	225g (8oz)	8 min	Stir or shake during cooking;
	450g (1lb)	11–12 min	stand 3 min before serving
green, sliced	225g (8oz)	7–8 min	Stir during cooking;
or whole	450g (1lb)	11–12 min	stand 2–3 min before serving
Broccoli spears	225g (8oz)	8–9 min	Rearrange spears during cooking;
	450g (1lb)	10–11 min	stand 2–3 min before serving
Brussels sprouts	225g (8oz)	6–7 min	Stir or shake during cooking;
	450g (1lb)	9–10 min	stand 2 min before serving
Carrots	225g (8oz)	7–8 min	Stir or shake during cooking;
	450g (1lb)	11–12 min	stand 2 min before serving
Cauliflower, florets	225g (8oz)	7–8 min	Separate during cooking;
	450g (1lb)	11–12 min	stand 2 min before serving
Corn-on-the-cob	1 cob	4 min	Wrap in buttered greaseproof paper;
	2 cobs	7 min	no water; turn over during cooking
Mixed vegetables, diced	225g (8oz)	6 min	Stir during cooking; stand 2 min
	450g (1lb)	8–9 min	before serving
Peas	225g (8oz)	5–6 min	Stir or shake during cooking;
	450g (1lb)	7–9 min	stand 2 min before serving
Spinach, chopped or cut leaf	300g (10½oz) pack	9 min	Do not add water, add a knob of butter; stir during cooking; stand 2 min before serving
Stew pack	450g (1lb)	9–11 min	Stir during cooking; stand 3 min before serving
Sweetcorn	225g (8oz)	5–6 min	Stir during cooking; stand 2 min before serving

Ratatouille *(serves 4–6)*

225g (8oz) aubergines, sliced
salt
1 garlic clove, crushed or finely chopped
225g (8oz) onions, sliced
2×15ml tbsp (2tbsp) vegetable oil
225g (8oz) courgettes, sliced
1 red pepper, de-seeded and thinly sliced
1 green pepper, de-seeded and thinly sliced
225g (8oz) skinned tomatoes, fresh or canned,
    roughly chopped
1×15ml tbsp (1tbsp) tomato purée
salt and freshly ground black pepper
chopped parsley or chives

1 Sprinkle the sliced aubergines with salt and leave for 30 min. Rinse well, drain, and pat dry on absorbent kitchen paper.
2 Place the garlic, onions and oil in a large 2.8 litre (5pt) ovenproof casserole or bowl.
3 Cover with a tight-fitting lid or plastic wrap and cook on HIGH for 3 min.
4 Stir in the aubergines, courgettes and peppers.
5 Re-cover and cook on HIGH for 5 min.
6 Stir in the tomatoes, tomato purée and seasoning.
7 Re-cover and continue cooking on HIGH for 18 min, or until all the vegetables are tender. Stir two or three times during cooking.
8 Sprinkle with chopped parsley or chives.
9 Serve hot with meat or fish dishes, or cold as a starter or salad.

Cauliflower cheese *(serves 3–4)*

450g (1lb) fresh or frozen cauliflower florets
4×15ml tbsp (4tbsp) water
40g (1½oz) margarine
40g (1½oz) plain flour
300ml (½pt) milk
salt and pepper
100g (4oz) strong cheese, grated
paprika

1 Place the cauliflower florets and water in a flameproof casserole.
2 Cover with a tight-fitting lid or plastic wrap and microwave on HIGH for 5 min.

3 Shake or rearrange the florets and continue cooking, covered, on HIGH for a further 5 min.
4 Leave to stand, covered.
5 Meanwhile place the margarine in a Pyrex or ovenproof jug and microwave on HIGH for 1 min or until melted.
6 Blend in the flour, then gradually blend in the milk. Add seasoning.
7 Microwave on HIGH for 3½–4 min until sauce has boiled and thickened. Stir every 30 sec.
8 Stir in 50g (2oz) of the grated cheese.
9 Drain the cauliflower and coat with the sauce.
10 Sprinkle with remaining cheese and either brown under a preheated conventional grill or simply sprinkle with paprika, before serving.

Green beans amandine *(serves 4)*

450g (1lb) whole green beans, fresh or frozen
4×15ml tbsp (4tbsp) water
50g (2oz) blanched flaked almonds
50g (2oz) butter, flaked
salt and pepper

1 Place the beans and water in an ovenproof casserole.
2 Cover with a tight-fitting lid and microwave on HIGH for 5 min.
3 Stir or shake the beans and continue cooking, covered, on HIGH for a further 5 min or until just tender.
4 Leave to stand, covered, and keep warm.
5 Meanwhile, place the almonds and butter in a shallow ovenproof dish.
6 Microwave on HIGH for 6 min or until browned, stirring frequently.
7 Drain the beans, stir in the almonds and seasoning.
8 Reheat, covered, if necessary, on HIGH for 1½ min.

Parisienne potatoes *(serves 4)*

675g (1½lb) prepared weight, peeled large
   potatoes
4×15ml tbsp (4tbsp) water
50g (2oz) butter
2×15ml tbsp (2tbsp) vegetable oil

1 Using a round vegetable or melon baller, scoop small balls from the potatoes. Total weight of balls should be about 450g (1lb).
2 Place the potatoes with the water in an ovenproof casserole.
3 Cover with a tight-fitting lid or plastic wrap and microwave on HIGH for 6 min.
4 Drain the potato balls and dry thoroughly on kitchen paper.
5 Heat the butter and oil together in a frying-pan on a conventional cooker hob.
6 Fry the potato balls, turning them continually, until evenly browned.

Parsleyed new potatoes *(serves 3)*

450g (1lb) small new potatoes
4×15 tbsp (4tbsp) salted water
25g (1oz) butter
2×5ml tsp (2tsp) chopped parsley

1 Scrub the potatoes and prick all over with a fork.
2 Place the potatoes and water in an ovenproof casserole.
3 Cover with a tight-fitting lid or plastic wrap and microwave on HIGH for 5 min.
4 Stir, re-cover and microwave on HIGH for a further 3 min or until just tender. Do not overcook or the texture will be spongy.
5 Drain and leave to stand, covered.
6 Place the butter in a small Pyrex or ovenproof bowl and melt on HIGH for 30–45 sec. Stir in parsley.
7 Toss the potatoes in the parsley butter.

VARIATION
New potatoes in herb butter: substitute 2tsp freshly chopped mixed herbs for parsley.

Oven chips *(serves 2)*

350g (12oz) commercially prepared frozen oven chips

1 Preheat a microwave browning dish according to manufacturer's instructions. Time will depend on size of dish used.
2 Place the frozen chips in a single layer in the base of the preheated dish.
3 Microwave on HIGH for 2½–3 min.
4 Turn the chips over and cook on HIGH for about a further 2½–3 min.

Note:
1 *100g (4oz) frozen oven chips will require about 5 min total cooking time. Turn over after 2½ min.*
450g (1lb) frozen oven chips will require about 8 min total cooking time. Turn over after 3½ min.
2 *Actual time taken to brown and cook the chips will depend on the freezer storage temperature.*

Speedy 'roast' potatoes *(serves 4–6)*

675g (1½lb) prepared weight potatoes, cut into
   50g (2oz) pieces
4×15ml tbsp (4tbsp) salted water
oil for deep fat frying

1 Place the potatoes and water in a large ovenproof bowl or casserole.
2 Cover with a tight-fitting lid or plastic wrap and microwave on HIGH for 7 min.
3 Stir or shake the potatoes and continue cooking, covered, on HIGH for a further 7 min.
4 Stand, covered, for 3 min.
5 Drain thoroughly and brush with oil.
6 Deep-fat fry on the hob of a conventional cooker or in an electric deep-fat fryer, until golden brown and crisp.

Note:
1 *Never to deep-fat fry in a microwave oven.*
2 *The potatoes can be prepared in advance to step 5, then deep-fat fried when required.*

Browning dish fish cakes (page 45); Browning dish fish portions in batter (page 45); Oven chips (above)

Lyonnaise potatoes *(serves 4)*

25g (1oz) butter or margarine, flaked
225g (8oz) prepared weight onions, thinly sliced
3 × 15ml tbsp (3tbsp) milk
salt and pepper
450g (1lb) prepared weight potatoes, thinly sliced
chopped parsley or parsley sprigs

1 Place the butter or margarine with the onions in a shallow flameproof dish, about 1.1 litre (2pt) capacity.
2 Cover with plastic wrap and microwave on HIGH for 4 min or until onions are soft. Stir after 2 min.
3 Stir in milk and seasoning. Add the potato slices and coat in the milk and onion mixture.
4 Arrange the mixture in an even layer in the dish.
5 Cover with plastic wrap and microwave on HIGH for 6 min.
6 Gently stir and rearrange the mixture in an even layer.
7 Re-cover and microwave on HIGH for a further 6 min or until potatoes are tender when tested with a fork.
8 If preferred, top may be browned under a preheated conventional grill before serving sprinkled with chopped parsley or parsley sprigs.

Scalloped potatoes *(serves 3–4)*

450g (1lb) prepared weight potatoes, thinly sliced
salt and pepper
2 × 15ml tbsp (2tbsp) flour
25g (1oz) butter, flaked
150ml (¼pt) milk, approximately
paprika

1 Butter a 1.1 litre (2pt) flameproof dish or casserole and arrange a layer of potatoes in the base.
2 Sprinkle with salt and pepper, dredge with flour and dot with butter.
3 Repeat the layers.
4 Add enough milk so that it can just be seen through the top layer.

5 Cover with plastic wrap and microwave on HIGH for 6 min.
6 Stir gently, rearrange in an even layer, re-cover and microwave on HIGH for a further 6 min or until potatoes are tender.
7 Either stand, covered, for 5 min or brown under a preheated conventional grill, before serving sprinkled with paprika.

Boiled potatoes *(serves 3–4)*

450g (1lb) prepared weight potatoes
4 × 15ml tbsp (4tbsp) water

1 Cut the peeled potatoes into 25g (1oz) pieces and place with the water in an ovenproof casserole.
2 Cover with plastic wrap or a tight-fitting lid and microwave on HIGH for 10 min or until just tender when tested with a fork. Stir or shake at least once during the cooking period.
3 Stand, covered, for 2–3 min before serving.

VARIATION
Add a knob of butter, a little milk or cream, and mash the potatoes. Season to taste before serving.

Baked stuffed murphies *(serves 4)*

4 × 150–225g (6–8oz) potatoes
75g (3oz) streaky bacon rashers
75g (3oz) mature Cheddar, grated
a little milk
salt and pepper

1 Wash and dry the potatoes. Prick the skins, using a fork.
2 Arrange in a circle, at least 2.5cm (1in) apart, on kitchen paper on the floor of the oven.
3 Microwave on HIGH for 7 min.
4 Turn the potatoes over and continue cooking on HIGH for a further 7–8 min, depending on size.
5 Wrap in foil, shiny side in, and leave to stand for 5 min.
6 Meanwhile snip the bacon rind at regular intervals and arrange the rashers on

double-thickness crumpled kitchen paper, on a plate without metal trim. Cover lightly with kitchen paper.

7 Microwave on HIGH for 3½–4 min until bacon is crisp.

8 Remove paper immediately and chop bacon.

9 Unwrap the potatoes, cut a slice from the top of each one and carefully scoop out the flesh, reserving the shells.

10 Mix the cooked potato with most of the bacon and cheese, adding a little milk and seasoning to taste.

11 Pile the mixture back into the shells and top with remaining bacon and cheese.

12 Return the potatoes to the oven, arranging them as before in a circle, and reheat on HIGH for about 4 min.

Onion rings *(serves 2–3)*

1 or 2 onions weighing in total 225–250g (8–9oz) after peeling
2×15ml tbsp (2tbsp) water

1 Slice the onions into 0.6cm (¼in) thick slices and separate into rings.
2 Place the onion with the water in an ovenproof bowl or casserole.
3 Cover with a tight-fitting lid or plastic wrap and microwave on HIGH for 8 min or until tender. Stir or shake after 4 min.
4 Leave to stand for 2–3 min before serving.

VARIATION
The onion slices may be cooked in 2tbsp oil instead of water, if preferred. The oil should be heated on HIGH for 1 min before adding the onion rings. Toss the rings in the oil till well coated, cover the dish, and proceed as above.

Whole baked onions *(serves 4)*

4 onions, each weighing 75–100g (3–4oz)
butter

1 Peel the onions, remove the root end, and cut a slice from the top.

2 Arrange the onions in a circle in an ovenproof dish, and top each with a knob of butter.
3 Cover the dish with plastic wrap and microwave on HIGH for 6 min.
4 Rearrange the onions in the dish, re-cover and continue cooking on HIGH for about a further 6 min.
5 Leave to stand, covered, for 2–3 min before serving.

Note: *2×75–100g (3–4oz) onions will require a total cooking time of about 8 min on* HIGH.

Leeks in cheese sauce *(serves 4)*

450g (1lb) prepared weight leeks, thickly sliced
4×15ml tbsp (4tbsp) water
25g (1oz) margarine
25g (1oz) plain flour
300ml (½pt) milk
salt and pepper
75g (3oz) red Cheddar or red Leicester cheese, grated
pinch of cayenne
a little made mustard
paprika or imitation bacon chiplets

1 Place the leeks and water in a shallow ovenproof dish.
2 Cover with a tight-fitting lid or plastic wrap and microwave on HIGH for 9 min, stirring after every 3 min.
3 Leave to stand, covered.
4 Place the margarine in a Pyrex or ovenproof jug and microwave on HIGH for 45 sec or until melted.
5 Blend in flour, then gradually blend in the milk. Add seasoning.
6 Microwave on HIGH for 3½–4 min until sauce has boiled and thickened. Stir or whisk every minute, and at the end of the cooking period.
7 Stir in the cheese, cayenne and mustard, mixing well.
8 Drain the leeks, pour the sauce over, cover and heat on HIGH for about 1½ min.
9 Sprinkle with paprika or imitation bacon chiplets before serving.

Tuna stuffed peppers
(serves 4 as a main meal: 8 as a starter)

4 medium green or red peppers
4×15ml tbsp (4tbsp) water
1×227g (8oz) can tomatoes
1×185g (6½oz) can tuna chunks in vegetable oil, drained
25g (1oz) brown breadcrumbs
2×15ml tbsp (2tbsp) grated cheese, optional
salt and pepper

1 Cut the peppers in half lengthwise and remove cores and seeds.
2 Arrange the peppers in a single layer in a large shallow ovenproof dish. Add the water.
3 Cover with plastic wrap and microwave on HIGH for 3 min.
4 Rearrange the peppers in the dish, re-cover and microwave on HIGH for a further 3 min.
5 Leave to stand, covered, while preparing the filling.
6 Chop the tomatoes roughly. Place them with 2tbsp of their juice in a mixing bowl. Stir in the tuna chunks, breadcrumbs, cheese if used, and seasoning to taste. Mix well together.
7 Drain most of the water from the peppers.
8 Stuff the peppers with the tuna mixture.
9 Cover the dish and microwave on LOW for 10 min.
10 Serve hot or cold with salad.

Honey-glazed carrots *(serves 4)*

450g (1lb) prepared weight carrots, sliced 1.25cm (½in) thick
2×15ml tbsp (2tbsp) water
15g (½oz) butter
pinch of ground cinnamon
1×15ml tbsp (1tbsp) clear honey
2×15ml tbsp (2tbsp) chopped walnuts, optional

1 Place the carrots and water in an ovenproof casserole.
2 Cover with a tight-fitting lid or plastic wrap and microwave on HIGH for 6 min.

3 Stir, re-cover and cook on HIGH for a further 6 min.
4 Stand, covered, for 2 min.
5 Drain the carrots and stir in the butter and cinnamon.
6 Drizzle with honey, re-cover, and microwave on HIGH for 30 sec.
7 Sprinkle with chopped walnuts, if used, before serving.

VARIATION
Cranberry glazed carrots: replace honey with 2tbsp cranberry jelly. Toss the cooked carrots in the jelly, re-cover and microwave on HIGH for 30 sec to melt the jelly.

Courgettes Gruyère *(serves 4)*

450g (1lb) courgettes, sliced
salt and freshly ground black pepper
75g (3oz) grated Gruyère cheese
paprika

1 Place the courgettes in an ovenproof casserole. Do not add water.
2 Cover with a tight-fitting lid or plastic wrap and microwave on HIGH for 5 min.
3 Stir, re-cover, and continue cooking on HIGH for a further 4 min or until courgettes are crisp but tender. Do not overcook.
4 Drain the courgettes, add seasoning, and arrange in an even layer in the casserole.
5 Top with the grated cheese.
6 Microwave on HIGH for 1–1½ min until cheese has started to melt.
7 Brown under a preheated conventional grill if preferred.
8 Sprinkle with paprika before serving.

Tuna stuffed peppers (above); Honey-glazed carrots with walnuts (above); Courgettes Gruyère (above)

Cabbage wedges *(serves 3–4)*

½ firm cabbage, weighing about 450g (1lb)
4 × 15ml tbsp (4tbsp) water

1 Cut cabbage into 3 or 4 wedges and remove core.
2 Place the wedges and the water in an oven-proof casserole with the core ends towards the centre of the dish.
3 Cover with a tight-fitting lid or plastic wrap and microwave on HIGH for 5 min.
4 Turn wedges over, re-cover, and continue cooking on HIGH for a further 5 min or until tender but crisp.
5 Stand, covered, for 2 min before draining and serving.

Bavarian red cabbage *(serves 4)*

450g (1lb) red cabbage, finely shredded
1 medium onion, peeled and sliced
1 large cooking apple, peeled, cored and sliced
2 × 15ml tbsp (2tbsp) brown sugar
pinch of ground cloves
pinch of ground cinnamon
salt and freshly ground pepper
4 × 15ml tbsp (4tbsp) red wine vinegar
1 bayleaf

1 Place all the ingredients in a 2 litre (3½pt) ovenproof bowl or casserole and stir well to mix.
2 Cover with plastic wrap or a tight-fitting lid and microwave on HIGH for 20 min or until cooked, stirring three times during this period.
3 Remove bayleaf and check seasoning before serving.

Stuffed cabbage leaves *(serves 4)*

1 medium cabbage
2 × 15ml tbsp (2tbsp) water
1 large onion, peeled and finely chopped
1 × 15ml tbsp (1tbsp) vegetable oil
350 (12oz) cooked beef or ham, minced
100g (4oz) beansprouts
2 × 15ml tbsp (2tbsp) tomato purée
salt and pepper
1 × 397g (14oz) can tomatoes with their juice
1 × 5ml tsp (1tsp) dried oregano

1 Discard the tough outer cabbage leaves and select 8 large perfect ones. Reserve remaining cabbage for another meal.
2 Remove any hard centre ribs from the leaves.
3 Place the leaves with the water in a large ovenproof bowl, cover with plastic wrap and cook on HIGH for 5 min or until soft. Drain and set aside.
4 Place the onion with the oil in an ovenproof bowl, cover and cook on HIGH for 4 min or until soft.
5 Stir in the minced beef or ham, beansprouts, tomato purée and seasoning.
6 Divide the mixture among the leaves, placing it in the centre of each leaf.
7 Fold the sides of the leaves towards the centre and roll up firmly. If necessary, secure in position with wooden cocktail sticks.
8 Place in a single layer in an ovenproof dish.
9 Pour over the tomatoes and their juice. Sprinkle with oregano.
10 Cover and cook on HIGH for 3 min. Reduce to LOW setting and continue cooking for a further 5–6 min until filling is hot.

Vichy carrots *(serves 4)*

450g (1lb) prepared weight carrots, sliced if old, left whole if young baby carrots
4 × 15ml tbsp (4tbsp) salted water
25g (1oz) butter, cut into small pieces
1 × 5ml tsp (1tsp) caster sugar
knob of butter
freshly ground black pepper
chopped parsley

1 Place the carrots, water, 25g (1oz) butter and sugar in an ovenproof casserole. Stir well to mix.
2 Cover with a lid or plastic wrap and micro-wave on HIGH for 5 min.
3 Stir, re-cover and continue cooking on HIGH for a further 4–5 min, depending on age of carrots.

4 Uncover and cook on HIGH for 1–2 min until the water has evaporated.
5 Stir in the knob of butter until melted.
6 Season with freshly ground black pepper and sprinkle with chopped parsley before serving.

Spicy sprouts *(serves 4)*

450g (1lb) prepared weight Brussels sprouts
4 × 15ml tbsp (4tbsp) water
25g (1oz) butter
½ × 5ml tsp (½tsp) grated nutmeg

1 Cut a cross in the stalk of the prepared sprouts and place them with the water in an ovenproof casserole.
2 Cover with a tight-fitting lid or plastic wrap and cook on HIGH for 5 min.
3 Stir or shake the sprouts and continue cooking, covered, for a further 5 min or until just cooked.
4 Stand for 3 min before draining.
5 Toss the drained sprouts in the butter and nutmeg.

Piquant tomatoes *(serves 2)*

4 tomatoes, total weight about 225g (8oz), cut in half horizontally
60ml (2fl oz) mayonnaise
2 × 5ml tsp (2tsp) chive mustard, or to taste
paprika

1 Arrange the tomato halves on a large round ovenproof plate without metal trim, preferably in a circle around the outside.
2 Mix the mayonnaise with the mustard, to taste, and spread on the tomatoes.
3 Microwave on HIGH for 4 min, rearranging the tomatoes, if necessary, after 2 min.
4 Stand for 1 min before serving with fish or ham.

Buttered swede *(serves 4)*

450g (1lb) prepared weight swede, thickly peeled and diced
4 × 15ml tbsp (4tbsp) water
salt and pepper
grated nutmeg, optional
40g (1½oz) butter, flaked
chopped parsley

1 Place the diced swede and water in a large ovenproof bowl or casserole.
2 Cover with plastic wrap and microwave on HIGH for 6 min.
3 Stir or shake and continue cooking, covered, on HIGH for a further 6 min or until tender.
4 Leave to stand, covered, for 5 min.
5 Drain and mash with salt and pepper, nutmeg if used, and butter.
6 Serve sprinkled with finely chopped parsley.

Note: *Actual cooking time will depend on age and quality of swede. It is important to peel swede thickly to completely remove all the tough outer skin. Cook as soon as possible after peeling.*

Baked celery cheese *(serves 4)*

350g (12oz) celery, sliced
3 × 15ml tbsp (3tbsp) water
25g (1oz) margarine
25g (1oz) plain flour
300ml (½pt) milk
salt and pepper
75g (3oz) grated cheese
3 × 15ml tbsp (3tbsp) brown breadcrumbs

1 Place the celery and water in an ovenproof dish.
2 Cover and cook on HIGH for 10 min or until tender, stirring or shaking after 5 min.
3 Leave to stand, covered, for 5 min.
4 Meanwhile melt the margarine in an ovenproof jug on HIGH for 1 min.
5 Stir in the flour and gradually blend in the milk.
6 Cook on HIGH for 3–4 min until sauce has thickened, stirring every minute.
7 Season sauce to taste and stir in grated cheese.
8 Drain the celery.
9 Layer the celery and sauce, finishing with sauce, in a 1.1 litre (2pt) pie dish.
10 Sprinkle the breadcrumbs on top and reheat on HIGH for 2 min.

Sauces

Sauces are quick and easy to make, provided they are stirred frequently during cooking to avoid lumps, just as when cooked conventionally. The great advantage of making sauces in a microwave oven is that there is less risk of sticking or scorching, and they can be cooked in advance and reheated in an ovenproof sauceboat. You can measure, mix and cook sauces in an ovenproof measuring jug, but do be sure to choose one large enough to prevent spillage when the sauce boils.

Basic white sauce *(makes 300ml/½pt)*

25g (1oz) margarine
25g (1oz) plain flour
300ml (½pt) milk
salt and pepper

1 Place margarine in a Pyrex or ovenproof jug of at least 600ml (1pt) capacity.
2 Microwave on HIGH for about 45 sec or until melted.
3 Blend in the flour, then gradually blend in the milk.
4 Microwave on HIGH for 3½–4 min or until sauce has boiled and thickened. Stir or whisk every minute and at the end of the cooking period. Do not leave metal utensils in the oven.
5 Season to taste before serving.

VARIATIONS
Cheese sauce: add 75g (3oz) grated cheese, a pinch of cayenne pepper, and a little made mustard to the thickened sauce. Microwave on HIGH for a further 30 sec, stir well and serve.
Egg sauce: add a finely chopped hard-boiled egg to the thickened sauce.
Mushroom sauce: add 50g (2oz) finely chopped mushrooms to the sauce for the final 2 min of the cooking period.
Parsley sauce: add 1–2tbsp chopped parsley to the thickened sauce.

Apple sauce *(makes about 300ml/½pt)*

450g (1lb) prepared weight of cooking apples, thinly sliced
3 × 15ml tbsp (3tbsp)
25g (1oz) butter
sugar if necessary

1 Place the apples and water in an ovenproof casserole.
2 Cover with a tight-fitting lid or plastic wrap and microwave on HIGH for 3 min.
3 Stir well, re-cover and continue cooking on HIGH for a further 3 min or until the apples are very soft.
4 Beat with a wooden spoon, then sieve or purée in an electric blender.
5 Stir in the butter and add a little sugar if the apples are tart.
6 Serve hot or cold with pork, duck or goose.

Roast duckling garnished with watercress (page 61); Apple sauce (above); Parisienne potatoes (page 70); Orange and cress salad

Giblet gravy *(makes 450ml/¾pt)*

giblets from a chicken or turkey
450ml (¾pt) warm water
1½×15ml tbsp (1½tbsp) cornflour
salt and pepper
gravy browning if necessary

1 Prick the livers and cut in half.
2 Place the giblets with the water in a deep 2.8 litre (5pt) ovenproof bowl.
3 Cover with plastic wrap and microwave on HIGH for at least 20 min. Strain the stock into an ovenproof jug.
4 Add strained juices from the cooked poultry, or water, to give 450ml (¾pt) stock.
5 Blend the cornflour to a smooth paste with a little cold water. Stir into the stock.
6 Microwave on HIGH for 3 min or until gravy has boiled and thickened. Stir every minute. Time taken to boil will depend on temperature of stock used.
7 Season to taste and add a little gravy browning if necessary.

Meat gravy *(makes 300ml/½pt)*

1×15ml tbsp (1tbsp) cornflour
3×15ml tbsp (3tbsp) meat juices
300ml (½pt) hot stock
salt and pepper
gravy browning if necessary

1 Blend the cornflour with the meat juices in a Pyrex or ovenproof jug.
2 Blend in the hot stock.
3 Microwave on HIGH for 2–3 min or until gravy boils, stirring every minute.
4 Add seasoning to taste and stir in a little gravy browning if necessary.
5 Strain into a heated gravy boat.

Bread sauce *(makes 300ml/½pt)*

1 small onion, peeled and stuck with 2 cloves
1 bayleaf
3 peppercorns, optional
300ml (½pt) milk
50g (2oz) breadcrumbs
15g (½oz) butter
salt and pepper
extra butter, optional

1 Place the onion, cloves, bayleaf, peppercorns and milk in a Pyrex or ovenproof jug.
2 Microwave on HIGH for 3 min. Leave to stand, covered, for at least 10 min to infuse. Uncover.
3 Stir in the breadcrumbs and 15g (½oz) butter, and cook on HIGH for 4 min.
4 Remove the onion, cloves, bayleaf and peppercorns and beat sauce well. Season to taste.
5 Beat in an extra 15g (½oz) butter, if necessary.
6 Serve with chicken or turkey.

Cranberry sauce *(makes about 300ml/½pt)*

250g (8oz) cranberries
150g (6oz) caster sugar
60ml (2fl oz) water or orange juice

1 Place the ingredients in an ovenproof bowl.
2 Cover with plastic wrap and microwave on HIGH for 2 min.
3 Stir, re-cover and continue cooking on HIGH for a further 2–3 min or until the skins on the cranberries pop.
4 Leave to stand, covered, for 5 min.
5 Serve hot or cold with roast turkey or chicken.

Note:
1 *If a thicker sauce is preferred, reduce to LOW setting after step 3 and continue cooking for about 10 min, stirring at least twice during this time.*
2 *If a smooth sauce is preferred, purée in a food processor or blender.*

Béchamel sauce *(makes 300ml/½pt)*

1 small onion, peeled and stuck with 6 cloves
½ small carrot, peeled and sliced
½ stick celery, sliced
1 bayleaf
3 peppercorns, optional
300ml (½pt) milk
25g (1oz) margarine
25g (1oz) plain flour
salt and pepper

1 Place the onion, carrot, celery, bayleaf and peppercorns with the milk in an ovenproof bowl.
2 Microwave on HIGH for 3 min. Leave to stand, covered, for at least 10 min, to infuse.
3 Place margarine in a Pyrex or ovenproof jug of at least 600ml (1pt) capacity. Microwave on HIGH for 30 sec or until melted.
4 Blend in the flour, then gradually blend in the strained milk.
5 Microwave on HIGH for 2–2½ min or until sauce thickens. Stir or whisk during cooking. Do not leave metal utensils in the oven.
6 Add seasoning before serving.

Sweet and sour sauce
(makes about 240ml/8fl oz)

120ml (4fl oz) pineapple juice
60ml (2fl oz) distilled malt vinegar
50g (2oz) soft brown sugar
2×15ml tbsp (2tbsp) vegetable oil
2×5ml tsp (2tsp) soy sauce

1 Place the ingredients in a Pyrex or ovenproof jug.
2 Microwave on HIGH for 1 min.
3 Stir well and microwave for a further 1½ min or until sauce boils, stirring after 1 min.
4 Serve with fish, poultry or vegetables.

Onion sauce *(makes about 450ml/¾pt)*

1 or 2 onions, total weight 225g (8oz), peeled and finely chopped
25g (1oz) margarine
25g (1oz) plain flour

300ml (½pt) milk
salt and pepper

1 Place onion and margarine in a Pyrex or ovenproof jug.
2 Cover with plastic wrap and microwave on HIGH for 5 min, stirring or shaking after 2½ min.
3 Blend in the flour until smooth, then gradually blend in the milk. Add seasoning.
4 Microwave on HIGH for 3½ min or until sauce has boiled and thickened. Stir every minute. Do not leave metal utensils in the oven.
5 Serve with roast lamb or mutton.

Sabayon sauce *(makes about 150ml/¼pt)*

3 egg yolks
75g (3oz) caster sugar
a few drops of vanilla essence
3×15ml tbsp (3tbsp) Marsala or, if unavailable, sweet sherry

1 Beat the egg yolks and sugar together in an ovenproof bowl. Stir in the essence.
2 Microwave on LOW for about 5 min or until sauce thickens. Whisk well every minute. Do not leave whisk in oven.
3 Whisk in sherry.
4 Serve hot or cold on its own or with fruit desserts or steamed fruit puddings, including Christmas pudding.

Brandy sauce *(makes 300ml/½pt)*

1×15ml tbsp (1tbsp) cornflour
300ml (½pt) milk
2×15ml tbsp (2tbsp) caster sugar
2×15ml tbsp (2tbsp) brandy

1 Blend the cornflour with a little of the measured milk in a Pyrex or ovenproof jug.
2 Gradually blend in remaining milk and stir in sugar.
3 Microwave on HIGH for 3½ min or until sauce has boiled and thickened. Stir every minute. Do not leave metal utensils in the oven.
4 Stir in brandy.
5 Serve hot with Christmas pudding.

Chocolate sauce *(makes 300ml/½pt)*

1×15ml tbsp (1tbsp) cocoa, sieved
2×5ml tsp (2tsp) cornflour
300ml (½pt) milk
25g (1oz) caster or soft brown sugar
knob of butter, optional

1 Place the cocoa and cornflour in a Pyrex or ovenproof jug of at least 600ml (1pt) capacity.
2 Blend to a smooth paste with a little of the measured milk.
3 Blend in remaining milk. Stir in sugar.
4 Microwave on HIGH for 3½ min or until sauce has boiled and thickened. Stir every minute. Do not leave metal utensils in oven.
5 Stir in butter, if used.
6 Serve hot with baked or steamed puddings.

Note: *Substitute 1tbsp chocolate-flavoured cornflour for the cocoa and cornflour, if preferred.*

Pineapple sauce *(makes about 450ml/¾pt)*

3×5ml tsp (3tsp) cornflour
1×439g (15½oz) can crushed pineapple
3×15ml tbsp (3 tbsp) demerara sugar
2×5ml tsp (2tsp) white vinegar
1×15ml tbsp (1tbsp) tomato ketchup

1 Blend the cornflour to a smooth paste with a little of the Pineapple juice.
2 Stir into remaining ingredients in an ovenproof bowl.
3 Cover and microwave on HIGH for 3½–4 min or until sauce boils and thickens. Stir every minute.
4 Serve hot or cold with pork or ham, or poured over a cooked bacon joint.

Rum butter sauce *(makes about 450ml/¾pt)*

1×15ml tbsp (1tbsp) cornflour
225g (8oz) caster sugar
180ml (6fl oz) half-cream or creamy milk
100g (4oz) butter, cut into small pieces
1–2×15ml tbsp (1–2tbsp) rum

1 Place the cornflour and sugar in a 1.1 litre (2pt) Pyrex or ovenproof bowl.
2 Blend in the cream gradually. Add the butter.
3 Microwave on HIGH for 3 min.
4 Stir well and microwave on HIGH for a further 3½ min or until sauce has boiled for 2 min and has thickened slightly.
5 Stir in rum and serve with ice-cream or sponge puddings.

VARIATIONS
Replace rum with brandy and serve sauce with Christmas pudding.

Egg custard sauce *(makes 300ml/½pt)*

300ml (½pt) milk
2 egg yolks or 1 whole egg
25g (1oz) caster sugar
few drops vanilla essence

1 Place milk in a Pyrex or ovenproof jug and heat on HIGH for 2 min.
2 Beat the egg and sugar together, stir in the strained heated milk.
3 Stir in vanilla essence and microwave the sauce on LOW for 4 min or until creamy. Do not allow sauce to boil, or it will curdle.
4 Use as a pouring custard over desserts or fruit.

Note: *If a slightly thicker sauce is preferred, blend 15g (½oz) cornflour with the milk before heating.*

Chicken curry (page 60); Brown rice (page 88)

Fresh fruit sauce
(makes about 180ml/6fl oz)

1 × 5ml tsp (1tsp) arrowroot
1 × 15ml tbsp (1tbsp) natural unsweetened
  orange juice
225g (8oz) raspberries or strawberries
50g–75g (2oz–3oz) caster sugar, or to taste.

1 Blend the arrowroot with the orange juice
  and place in a large ovenproof bowl, 2.8 litre
  (5pt) capacity, with the fruit.
2 Microwave on HIGH for 2 min.
3 Stir in the sugar, stirring until dissolved.
4 Microwave on HIGH for a further 2 min.
5 Serve hot or cold with baked or steamed puddings, meringue sweets, a cold soufflé or ice-
  cream.

Jam sauce *(makes about 450ml/$\frac{3}{4}$pt)*

300ml ($\frac{1}{2}$pt) water
4 good × 15ml tbsp (4tbsp) jam
1 heaped × 5ml tsp (1tsp) arrowroot
lemon juice to taste

1 Place water in an ovenproof measuring jug
  and microwave on HIGH for 2 min. Stir in jam.
2 Blend the arrowroot with a little cold water
  and stir into the sauce.
3 Microwave on HIGH for 2–2$\frac{1}{2}$ min, stirring
  every minute.
4 Add lemon juice to taste.
5 Sieve sauce if jam has seeds.

VARIATION
Marmalade sauce: substitute marmalade for
jam and proceed as above. Do not sieve.

Butterscotch sauce *(makes about 150ml/$\frac{1}{4}$pt)*

50g (2oz) butter
4 × 15ml tbsp (4tbsp) soft brown sugar
2 × 15ml tbsp (2tbsp) golden syrup
2 × 15ml tbsp (2tbsp) chopped nuts, optional
squeeze of lemon juice

1 Place the butter, sugar and syrup in a Pyrex
  measuring jug or bowl and microwave on
  HIGH for 45 sec.
2 Stir well and microwave on HIGH for a further
  45 sec.
3 Stir well until sugar has completely dissolved.
4 Microwave on HIGH for a further 1$\frac{1}{2}$–2 min or
  until sauce has thickened, stirring every
  minute.
5 Stir in nuts, if used, and lemon juice.
6 Serve hot over ice-cream or baked apples.

Orange liqueur sauce *(makes 300ml/$\frac{1}{2}$pt)*

1 × 15ml tbsp (1 tbsp) cornflour
240ml (8fl oz) natural unsweetened orange juice
3 × 15ml tbsp (3tbsp) Cointreau, Grand
  Marnier or Mandarine Napoleon liqueur
sugar to taste

1 Blend the cornflour to a smooth paste with a
  little of the measured orange juice, in a Pyrex
  or ovenproof jug of at least 600ml (1pt)
  capacity.
2 Blend in remaining juice.
3 Microwave on HIGH until sauce has boiled
  and thickened. Stir every minute.
4 Stir in liqueur and add sugar to taste.
5 Serve with ice-cream, fruit, soufflé or steamed
  pudding.

Rice and pasta

Cooking rice and pasta takes virtually as long by microwave as it does by conventional methods. This is because they are dried products and require time to absorb moisture. However, they require less attention when they are cooked in the microwave oven, and the amount of steam in the kitchen is greatly reduced compared with conventional cooking. Rice is less likely to stick, and there is no dirty saucepan to clean at the end of the cooking period.

If your oven will simmer on LOW setting, rice and pasta can be cooked on this setting, after initially bringing to a rolling boil on HIGH. Always cook rice and pasta in a very large covered bowl to avoid spillage. Cooked rice reheats beautifully in a microwave oven. Simply add about 2 tablespoons of water to create some steam, cover and reheat the rice on HIGH for a few minutes, depending on quantity. Stir gently during this period.

Guide to cooking rice and pasta

Food	Quantity	Preparation	Approximate Time on HIGH Setting	Standing Time
American, long-grain, or Patna rice	225g (8oz)	Place in a large ovenproof bowl with 480ml (16fl oz) boiling salted water and 1 × 15ml tbsp (1 tbsp) oil; cover	15 min	5 min
Brown rice	225g (8oz)	Place in a large ovenproof bowl with 600ml (1pt) boiling salted water and 1 × 15ml tbsp (1 tbsp) oil; cover	25–26 min	5 min
Macaroni	225g (8oz)	Place in a large ovenproof bowl with 600ml (1pt) boiling salted water and 1 × 15ml tbsp (1 tbsp) oil; cover	10–12 min	3 min
Noodles	225g (8oz)	Place in a large ovenproof bowl with 600ml (1pt) boiling salted water and 1 × 15ml tbsp (1 tbsp) oil; cover	8 min	2 min

Food	Quantity	Preparation	Approximate Time on HIGH Setting	Standing Time
Pasta shells, shapes	225g (8oz)	Place in a large ovenproof bowl with 900ml (1½pt) boiling salted water and 1×15ml tbsp (1tbsp) oil; cover	12–15 min	3 min
Spaghetti	225g (8oz)	Lower into a large ovenproof bowl with 1 litre (1¾pt) boiling salted water and 1×15ml tbsp (1tbsp) oil; cover	12 min	2 min

Note: In some ovens it is possible to simmer rice and pasta on LOW setting. If so, cook on HIGH only until the rice or pasta is boiling and then reduce to LOW setting and continue cooking for time given in chart above. This helps to reduce the risk of spillage.

Tagliatelle romano *(serves 4)*

225g (8oz) tagliatelle or tagliatelle verde
900ml (1½pt) boiling water
1×5ml tsp (1tsp) salt
1×15ml tbsp (1tbsp) vegetable oil
25g (1oz) butter, flaked
225g (8oz) mushrooms, sliced
1×298g (10½oz) can condensed cream of
  mushroom soup, undiluted
100g (4oz) cooked ham, chopped
salt and pepper
grated Parmesan cheese, optional

1 Place the tagliatelle, water, salt and oil in a large 2.8 litre (5pt) ovenproof bowl.
2 Cover and microwave on HIGH for 8 min. Leave to stand, covered.
3 Place the butter and mushrooms in an ovenproof bowl. Cover and microwave on HIGH for 3 min.
4 Mix the soup with the cooking liquor from the mushrooms, cover and microwave on HIGH for 3½ min or until just boiling.
5 Stir the soup into the drained tagliatelle, then stir in the ham and mushrooms. Season to taste.
6 Cover and heat on HIGH for about 1½ min.
7 Serve with grated Parmesan if used.

VARIATION
Substitute condensed cream of chicken soup for mushroom soup, and replace cooked ham with cooked chicken.

Spaghetti alla carbonara *(serves 4)*

1 litre (1¾pt) boiling water
1×15ml tbsp (1tbsp) vegetable oil
1×5ml tsp (1tsp) salt
225g (8oz) spaghetti
4 rashers streaky bacon
25g (1oz) butter
1×15ml tbsp (1tbsp) vegetable oil
3 eggs, beaten
50g (2oz) grated Parmesan cheese
100g (4oz) cooked ham, chopped
salt and pepper
3×15ml tbsp (3tbsp) grated Parmesan cheese

1 Place the water, oil and salt in a large 2.8 litre (5pt) ovenproof bowl.
2 Lower the spaghetti into the water and, as it softens, coil it round until it is completely submerged.
3 Cover with plastic wrap and microwave on HIGH for 12 min. Drain and leave to stand, covered.
4 Place bacon rashers in a shallow ovenproof dish. Cover with kitchen paper and microwave on HIGH for 4 min or until crisp. Drain and crumble.
5 Place the butter and oil in a large ovenproof casserole and microwave on HIGH for 1 min or until butter is melted.

Tagliatelle romano (above); Spaghetti alla carbonara (above)

6 Whisk eggs into butter and oil. Stir in spaghetti, 50g (2oz) Parmesan, ham and crumbled bacon. Season to taste.
7 Microwave on HIGH for $3\frac{1}{2}$ min or until eggs are set. Stir every minute.
8 Serve immediately, sprinkled with remaining grated cheese, accompanied by salad.

Boiled long-grain rice *(serves 4)*

480ml (16fl oz) boiling water or chicken stock
225g (8oz) long-grain rice
1×5ml tsp (1tsp) salt
1×15ml tbsp (1tbsp) oil, optional

1 Pour the boiling water or stock into a large 2.8 litre (5pt) ovenproof bowl.
2 Stir in the rice, salt and oil if used.
3 Cover with plastic wrap and microwave on HIGH for 2–3 min or until boiling.
4 Reduce setting to LOW (see Note 2) and continue cooking for a further 15 min or until rice is just cooked and water has been absorbed. Stir at least once during this time.
5 Leave to stand, covered, for at least 5 min to finish cooking before fluffing up with a fork to serve.

Note:
1 *If the rice has absorbed all the water before it is quite cooked, add 2tbsp boiling water and continue cooking.*
2 *If you find that the rice will not simmer on* LOW *setting on your oven, it should be cooked on* HIGH *setting throughout. The total cooking time on* HIGH *will be about 15 min. If cooking on* HIGH *throughout, it is advisable to add the oil, to help prevent spillage.*

VARIATION
Brown rice: use 600ml (1pt) boiling water. At step 3, microwave on HIGH for 2–3 min or until boiling. Either reduce setting to LOW and simmer for a further 25–30 min or continue cooking on HIGH for about a further 24 min. Leave to stand covered for at least 5 min before fluffing up with a fork to serve. Remember that brown rice has a slightly chewy texture and is never as soft as white rice.

Spaghetti bolognese *(serves 4)*

1 litre ($1\frac{3}{4}$pt) boiling water
1×15ml tbsp (1tbsp) vegetable oil
1×15ml tsp (1tsp) salt
225g (8oz) spaghetti
450g (1lb) lean minced beef
1 medium onion, peeled and finely chopped
1 garlic clove, minced or finely chopped
2×15ml tbsp (2tbsp) tomato purée
1×397g (14oz) can tomatoes
100g (4oz) mushrooms, sliced
1×5ml tsp (1tsp) dried mixed herbs
150ml ($\frac{1}{4}$pt) beef stock
salt and pepper

1 Place the boiling water, oil and salt in a large 2.8 litre (5pt) ovenproof bowl.
2 Lower the spaghetti into the water and, as it softens, coil it round in the bowl so that it is completely submerged.
3 Cover and cook on HIGH for 12 min. Leave to stand, covered.
4 Meanwhile crumble the minced beef and place with the onion and garlic in an ovenproof bowl or casserole. Cover and cook on HIGH for 5 min.
5 Break up mince with a fork and stir in the tomato purée, tomatoes, with their juice, mushrooms, herbs, stock and seasoning.
6 Cover and cook on HIGH for 15 min, stirring twice during this period.
7 Reheat the spaghetti on HIGH for about 3 min. Drain and place on a heated serving dish, topped with the meat sauce.

Chicken and ham risotto *(serves 4–6)*

1 medium onion, peeled and finely chopped
2×15ml tbsp (2tbsp) vegetable oil
225g (8oz) long-grain rice
3 tomatoes, skinned and roughly chopped
600ml (1pt) boiling chicken stock
225g (8oz) cooked chicken, diced
225g (8oz) cooked ham, diced
100g (4oz) canned or cooked peas
50g (2oz) sultanas or raisins
salt and pepper
grated Parmesan cheese
chopped parsley

1 Place the onion, oil and rice in a large 2.8 litre (5pt) ovenproof bowl.
2 Cover with plastic wrap and microwave on HIGH for 3 min.
3 Stir in the tomatoes and stock, re-cover and cook on HIGH for 15 min. Stir twice during cooking.
4 Stir in chicken, ham and peas. Re-cover and cook on HIGH for a further 3 min.
5 Stir in sultanas or raisins and season to taste.
6 Serve, sprinkled with grated Parmesan and chopped parsley.

VARIATION
Turkey risotto: substitute 450g (1lb) cooked diced turkey for the chicken and ham.

Seafood ring mould *(serves 4–6)*

100g (4oz) easy-cook rice
300ml (½pt) boiling water
½×5ml tsp (½tsp) salt
100g (4oz) diced frozen mixed vegetables
225g (8oz) white fish fillets
4×15ml tbsp (4tbsp) mayonnaise
100g (4oz) peeled prawns
2×5ml tsp (2tsp) tomato ketchup
fresh whole prawns, in their shells
lemon wedges

1 Place the rice, water and salt in a large 2 litre (3½pt) ovenproof bowl. Cover with plastic wrap and microwave on HIGH for 10 min.
2 Leave to stand, covered.
3 Place the frozen mixed vegetables in a small ovenproof bowl. Cover with plastic wrap and cook on HIGH for 3 min.
4 Place the fish on a large ovenproof plate, without metal trim, or in a shallow ovenproof dish.
5 Cover with plastic wrap and cook on HIGH for 3½ min.
6 Drain the cooked vegetables and stir into the rice. Bind together with 1tbsp mayonnaise.
7 Press this mixture into an oiled ring mould and refrigerate for about 1 hr.
8 Meanwhile drain and flake the cooked fish and stir in the peeled prawns.

9 Mix the remaining mayonnaise with the tomato ketchup and stir gently into the fish.
10 Stand the mould containing the rice in hot water for a few minutes. Place a serving plate over the mould and turn both upside down. Tap the mould and shake it a little to release the rice ring.
11 Fill the centre of the ring with the fish mixture.
12 Garnish with whole fresh prawns and serve chilled, with lemon wedges.

Tuna and cheese casserole *(serves 4)*

100g (4oz) pasta shells
600ml (1pt) boiling water
1×5ml tsp (1tsp) salt
1×15ml tbsp (1tbsp) vegetable oil
40g (1½oz) margarine
40g (1½oz) flour
450ml (¾pt) milk
salt and pepper
100g (4oz) strong cheese, grated
1×198g (7oz) can tuna fish, drained and flaked
1 medium tomato, sliced

1 Place the pasta, water, salt and oil in a large 2.8 litre (5pt) ovenproof bowl.
2 Cover and microwave on HIGH for 10 min. Leave to stand, covered.
3 Place the margarine in a large ovenproof jug and microwave on HIGH for 1¼ min or until melted.
4 Blend in the flour, then gradually blend in the milk. Add seasoning.
5 Microwave on HIGH for 4½ min or until sauce has boiled and thickened. Stir every minute.
6 Stir in half the cheese, the flaked tuna fish and the drained pasta.
7 Turn the mixture into a shallow flameproof casserole.
8 Microwave on HIGH for 3 min or until heated through.
9 Sprinkle with remaining cheese and brown under a preheated conventional grill.
10 Garnish with tomato slices before serving.

Kedgeree *(serves 4)*

150g (6oz) long-grain rice
360ml (12fl oz) boiling water
pinch of salt
350g (12oz) smoked haddock
50g (2oz) butter or margarine
1 medium onion, peeled and finely chopped
3 eggs, hard-boiled conventionally and shelled
salt and pepper
chopped parsley

1 Place the rice, water and salt in a large oven-proof bowl.
2 Cover with plastic wrap and microwave on HIGH for 15 min. Leave to stand, covered.
3 Meanwhile place the fish on an ovenproof plate or in a shallow ovenproof dish.
4 Cover with plastic wrap and microwave on HIGH for 3½ min or until tender.
5 Remove any skin or bones and flake the fish.
6 Place the butter or margarine in a large ovenproof dish and microwave on HIGH for 1 min.
7 Add the onion and cook on HIGH for 3 min.
8 Stir in the cooked rice, fish and two of the hard-boiled eggs, chopped. Season to taste.
9 Cover and heat on HIGH for about 3 min.
10 Slice remaining hard-boiled egg.
11 Garnish kedgeree with egg slices and chopped parsley before serving.

Spiced turkey pilau *(serves 4–6)*

1 medium onion, peeled and finely chopped
2×15ml tbsp (2tbsp) vegetable oil
225g (8oz) long-grain rice
480ml (16fl oz) boiling chicken stock
½×5ml tsp (½tsp) turmeric
¼×5ml tsp (¼tsp) ground cumin
¼×5ml tsp (¼tsp) ground coriander
salt and freshly ground black pepper
350–450g (12–16oz) cooked turkey, cubed
50g (2oz) raisins
50g (2oz) cashew nuts, optional

1 Place the onion, oil and rice in a large 2.8 litre (5pt) ovenproof bowl.

2 Cover and microwave on HIGH for 3 min.
3 Stir in the stock, turmeric, cumin, coriander, salt and pepper.
4 Cover with plastic wrap and cook on HIGH for 15 min.
5 Stir in the turkey and raisins, re-cover and cook on HIGH for a further 2 min.
6 Stir in nuts, if used, before serving with chopped cucumber mixed with natural unsweetened yoghurt.

Macaroni cheese *(serves 4)*

150g (6oz) short-cut macaroni
600ml (1pt) boiling water
½×5ml tsp (½tsp) salt
1×15ml tbsp (1tbsp) vegetable oil
40g (1½oz) margarine
40g (1½oz) plain flour
450ml (¾pt) milk
salt and pepper
pinch of cayenne
½×5ml tsp (½tsp) prepared mustard
150g (6oz) strong cheese, grated
1 tomato, sliced, optional

1 Place the macaroni, water, salt and oil in a large 2.8 litre (5pt) ovenproof bowl.
2 Cover with plastic wrap and microwave on HIGH for 10 min or until cooked but still firm. Leave to stand, covered.
3 Place the margarine in a large ovenproof jug and microwave on HIGH for 1¼ min or until melted.
4 Blend in the flour, then gradually blend in the milk.
5 Microwave on HIGH for 4½–5 min or until sauce has boiled and thickened.
6 Stir in salt, pepper, cayenne, mustard and 100g (4oz) cheese.
7 Drain the macaroni and coat with the sauce.
8 Turn into flameproof dish.
9 Sprinkle with remaining cheese.
10 Microwave on HIGH for 2 min or until cheese has melted. If preferred, brown under a preheated conventional grill.
11 Garnish with sliced tomato.

Chilli con carne (page 53); Pasta shapes

Eggs and cheese

Unless your oven manufacturer recommends a special way, do not try to cook eggs in their shells in a microwave oven. The rapid build up of pressure inside the shell will cause them to burst and explode. Eggs cook differently in a microwave oven than when cooked conventionally; the yolk cooks first, since it contains fat which attracts microwaves. Obviously when the yolks and the whites are beaten together, such as when cooking scrambled eggs, this does not happen. Try to use eggs at room temperature and always prick the membrane covering the yolk to prevent bursting during cooking.

Eggs cook rapidly in a microwave oven and should not be left unattended. Do not overcook, and remember that they will continue to cook after they are removed from the oven. Differences in egg sizes, as well as personal preference, will affect cooking times, so learn to remove them from the oven before they are completely cooked to your liking. Fried eggs are best cooked conventionally.

Cheese, like eggs, cooks very quickly by any method, but especially by microwave energy. Its high fat content attracts microwaves, so care must be taken to prevent overcooking, otherwise it will become tough and rubbery. If cheese is being used as a topping, remove the dish from the oven as soon as the cheese starts to melt. Always add cheese to dishes towards the end of the cooking time.

Baked eggs (serves 2)

2 eggs, at room temperature

1 Lightly butter 2 saucers without metal trim, or the insides of 2 ovenproof ramekin dishes.
2 Break an egg into each, and pierce the yolk carefully with a fork.
3 Cover with plastic wrap and microwave on LOW for $3\frac{1}{4}$–$3\frac{3}{4}$ min, depending on personal preference. Do not overcook.
4 Leave to stand, covered, for 1 min to finish cooking, before serving.

Note: *Instead of hard boiling eggs in their shells conventionally, bake as above and use or chop as required.*

Poached eggs (serves 2)

120ml (4fl oz) water
2×5ml tsp (2tsp) vinegar
2 eggs, at room temperature
2 slices bread, toasted conventionally and buttered

1 Select 2 ovenproof ramekin dishes or small dishes without metal trim and place 60ml (2fl oz) water and 1tsp vinegar in each.
2 Microwave on HIGH for 2 min or until boiling.
3 Carefully break the eggs into the dishes and pierce the yolks gently with a fork.
4 Microwave on HIGH for 1 min. Do not overcook.
5 Leave to stand to 1 min before draining and serving on hot buttered toast.

Swiss eggs (serves 2)

2 × 15ml tbsp (2tbsp) grated Gruyère cheese
2 eggs, at room temperature
2 × 15ml tbsp (2tbsp) double cream, optional
paprika

1 Lightly butter the insides of 2 ovenproof ramekin or individual small dishes without metal trim.
2 Sprinkle a little cheese in the bottom of the dishes.
3 Break the eggs on top and carefully pierce the yolks with a fork.
4 Pour 1tbsp of cream, if used, over each egg.
5 Sprinkle with remaining cheese.
6 Cover with plastic wrap and microwave on LOW for 3½–4 min, depending on personal preference. Do not overcook.
7 Leave to stand, covered, for 1 min to finish cooking before serving sprinkled with paprika.

VARIATIONS
1 Mix a little chopped skinned tomato with the cheese in the base of the dishes before breaking the eggs on top.
2 Halve the quantity of cheese and do not sprinkle any cheese in the base of the dishes. Instead, replace with 25g (1oz) finely chopped cooked ham. Break the eggs on top and proceed as above.
3 **Eggs en cocotte:** proceed as step 1 above. Omit the cheese and step 2 above. Proceed as step 3. Whip the cream until thick but not stiff. Stir in salt, pepper, garlic salt and paprika to taste. Spoon cream mixture over the eggs. Cover and cook on LOW for 3–3½ min. Stand and serve as step 7 above.

Egg Florentine (serves 1)

100g (4oz) frozen spinach
1 egg, at room temperature
1 × 15ml tbsp (1tbsp) grated cheese
salt and pepper
paprika

1 Place the frozen spinach in an ovenproof round serving dish.

2 Cover and cook on HIGH for 5 min. Drain and stir.
3 Make a depression in the centre of the spinach and break the egg into the well. Pierce the egg yolk carefully with a fork.
4 Re-cover and cook on LOW for 2–2½ min or until egg is set.
5 Sprinkle with grated cheese and microwave on HIGH for 30–45 sec or until cheese starts to melt.
6 Sprinkle with seasoning and paprika before serving.

Eggs mornay (serves 3)

6 eggs
25g (1oz) margarine
25g (1oz) plain flour
300ml (½pt) milk
salt and pepper
100g (4oz) grated cheese
chopped parsley

1 Hard boil the eggs in their shells conventionally for 10 min.
2 After they have been boiling for 5 min, prepare the sauce.
3 Place the margarine in a Pyrex or ovenproof jug and melt on HIGH for about 45 sec.
4 Blend in the flour and gradually blend in the milk.
5 Microwave on HIGH for 3½–4 min or until sauce has boiled and thickened.
6 Add seasoning and stir in 75g (3oz) of the cheese.
7 Shell and slice the hard-boiled eggs and place in a shallow flameproof dish.
8 Pour the sauce over the eggs and sprinkle the remaining cheese on top.
9 Brown under a preheated conventional grill.
10 Sprinkle with chopped parsley before serving.

Spanish omelette (serves 2–3)

25g (1oz) butter
1 small onion, peeled and finely chopped
½ small green pepper, de-seeded and chopped
½ small red pepper, de-seeded and chopped
1 medium potato, cooked and chopped
1×213g (7½oz) can mushrooms, drained and sliced
4 eggs, lightly beaten
salt and pepper

1 Place the butter in a shallow 22.5cm (9in) flameproof shallow round dish and microwave on HIGH for 45 sec or until melted.
2 Stir in the onion and peppers, cover and cook on HIGH for 3 min, stirring after 1½ min.
3 Add the potato and mushrooms. Stir in the beaten eggs and seasoning.
4 Cover with plastic wrap and microwave on HIGH for 1½ min.
5 Gently lift the cooked egg edges and allow the uncooked egg mixture to run underneath.
6 Re-cover and continue cooking on HIGH for a further 2 min or until mixture is set.
7 Remove plastic wrap and brown under a pre-heated conventional grill.
8 Serve cut in wedges.

Soufflé omelette (serves 2)

3 eggs, separated
3×15ml tbsp (3tbsp) water
salt and pepper
15g (½oz) butter

1 Whisk the egg whites until stiff but not dry.
2 In a separate bowl beat the egg yolks with the water and seasoning until thick.
3 Fold the beaten egg whites lightly into the yolk mixture. Do not overmix.
4 Place the butter in a 20–22.5cm (8–9in) round flameproof dish and microwave on HIGH for 30 sec or until melted.
5 Tilt the dish so that the inside is completely coated in melted butter.
6 Turn the egg mixture immediately into the dish and smooth lightly into an even layer.
7 Microwave on LOW for 5 min or until the omelette is just set.

8 Meanwhile preheat a conventional grill.
9 Brown the omelette immediately, folded or unfolded, under the hot grill.
10 Serve immediately.

VARIATION
Sweet omelette: omit salt and pepper and whisk egg whites with 25g (1oz) caster or sieved icing sugar. Add a few drops of vanilla essence to the beaten egg yolks. Spread the cooked omelette with warm jam or fruit purée after step 7 above and serve immediately, unfolded. Alternatively the omelette may be filled, folded and browned under an already preheated conventional grill as given above.

Browning dish breakfast (serves 2)

2 eggs, at room temperature
4 rashers bacon, de-rinded if preferred
knob of butter
2 medium tomatoes, halved

1 Break the eggs into saucers and pierce the yolks carefully with a fork. Snip the bacon fat at regular intervals to prevent curling.
2 Preheat a microwave browning dish according to manufacturer's instructions.
3 Immediately add the butter to the dish and place the bacon and tomatoes around the outside of the dish, pressing them down onto the hot surface.
4 Microwave on HIGH for 2 min.
5 Turn the bacon and tomatoes over and slide the eggs into the dish. Baste the eggs with bacon fat.
6 Cover dish with its lid and continue cooking on HIGH for about 2 min until eggs are set.
7 Leave to stand, covered, for 2 min to finish cooking, before serving.

Kipper (page 45); Kipper pâté (page 38); Kedgeree (page 90)

Ham and cheese omelette *(serves 2)*

4 eggs
2×15ml tbsp (2tbsp) water
2×15ml tbsp (2tbsp) chopped cooked ham
salt and pepper
25g (1oz) butter
1×15ml tbsp (1tbsp) grated cheese
chopped parsley

1 Beat the eggs and water together. Stir in the ham and seasoning.
2 Place the butter in a 22.5cm (9in) shallow round ovenproof dish and microwave on HIGH for 45 sec or until melted.
3 Tilt the dish to coat the base and sides with the melted butter.
4 Turn the egg mixture into the dish.
5 Cover with plastic wrap and microwave on HIGH for 1½ min.
6 Gently draw the cooked egg edges towards the centre of the dish and allow the uncooked mixture to run towards the outside.
7 Re-cover and cook on HIGH for a further 1 min.
8 Sprinkle the grated cheese over the surface and cook on HIGH for a further 30–45 sec or until cheese starts to melt.
9 Leave to stand for 1 min.
10 Sprinkle with chopped parsley before serving.

Cheese, onion and potato layer *(serves 3–4)*

450g (1lb) prepared weight potatoes
1 medium onion, peeled and grated
100–150g (4–6oz) grated cheese, preferably Gruyère
salt and pepper
150ml (¼pt) single cream or creamy milk
parsley sprigs or watercress

1 Lightly butter a shallow ovenproof dish.
2 Slice the potatoes very thinly and place a layer in the bottom of the dish.
3 Top with a little onion, cheese and seasoning.
4 Continue layering in this way, finishing with a layer of potatoes topped with cheese.

5 Pour over the cream or milk and cover with a tight-fitting lid or plastic wrap.
6 Microwave on HIGH for 6 min.
7 Uncover and microwave on HIGH for a further 6 min or until potatoes are cooked when tested with a fork.
8 Brown the top under a preheated conventional grill before serving garnished with parsley sprigs or watercress.

Cheese fondue *(serves 4–6)*

1 clove garlic, crushed
225g (8oz) Gruyère cheese, grated
225g (8oz) Emmenthal cheese, grated
1×15ml tbsp (1tbsp) cornflour
freshly ground black pepper
pinch of garlic powder
pinch of ground nutmeg
300ml (½pt) dry white wine
1 liqueur glass kirsch

1 Rub the garlic round the inside of a non-metallic fondue pot or deep ovenproof casserole.
2 Place the cheese, cornflour, pepper, garlic powder and nutmeg in a bowl and mix well together.
3 Pour the wine into the fondue pot or casserole and microwave on HIGH for 3–4 min until bubbles begin to appear; do not boil.
4 Stir in half the cheese mixture, mixing well together.
5 Microwave on HIGH for 2 min or until almost melted.
6 Stir well, then stir in remaining cheese mixture.
7 Microwave on HIGH for a further 2–3 min or until almost melted.
8 Whisk until smooth. Stir in kirsch. Microwave on LOW for 1 min.
9 Keep warm over a fondue burner or spirit lamp.
10 Serve with cubes of French bread or toasted wholemeal bread, button mushrooms and other raw vegetables to spear on fondue forks to dip into the fondue.

Cheese pudding (serves 3–4)

225g (8oz) wholemeal bread, crusts removed
150g (6oz) strong cheese, grated
3 eggs, beaten
450ml ($\frac{3}{4}$pt) milk
salt and pepper
$\frac{1}{4}$×5ml tsp ($\frac{1}{4}$tsp) mustard powder
paprika

1 Butter the inside of a 1.4 litre (2$\frac{1}{2}$pt) oven-proof soufflé dish.
2 Cut the bread into 1.25cm ($\frac{1}{2}$in) cubes, mix with 100g (4oz) of the cheese and place in the dish.
3 Beat together the eggs, milk, seasoning and mustard. Pour over the bread and cheese. Press bread into liquid.
4 Leave to stand for about 15 min, to allow the bread to soak up the liquid.
5 Press top surface with a fork to level. Sprinkle with remaining cheese.
6 Cover with plastic wrap and microwave on LOW for 15 min or until just set.
7 Brown top under a preheated conventional grill if preferred.
8 Sprinkle with paprika before serving.

Cheese, onion and tomato flan (serves 6)

25g (1oz) butter or margarine
450g (1lb) onions, peeled and thinly sliced
225g ($\frac{1}{2}$lb) tomatoes, skinned and chopped
100g (4oz) mature Cheddar cheese, grated
salt and pepper
1×22.5cm (9in) prebaked pastry flan case
paprika

1 Place butter or margarine and onions in an ovenproof casserole.
2 Cover and cook on HIGH for 7–9 min or until soft, stirring twice during cooking.
3 Stir in the tomatoes and most of the cheese. Season to taste.
4 Turn the mixture into the pastry case and sprinkle the remaining cheese on top.
5 Microwave on HIGH for 2–3 min or until the cheese has melted.
6 Sprinkle with paprika and serve warm or cold.

Cheese and vegetable flan (serves 4)

1×225g (8oz) pack frozen mixed vegetables
75g (3oz) mushrooms, sliced
25g (1oz) margarine
25g (1oz) plain flour
300ml ($\frac{1}{2}$pt) milk
salt and pepper
1 egg, beaten
75g (3oz) mature Cheddar cheese, grated
1×17.5cm (7in) pre-baked pastry flan case

1 Place the frozen vegetables in an ovenproof bowl with 2×15ml tbsp (2tbsp) water. Cover and microwave on HIGH for 5 min. Leave to stand, covered.
2 Place the mushrooms and margarine in an ovenproof bowl. Cover and cook on HIGH for 2 min.
3 Stir in the flour, blend in the milk and season.
4 Microwave on HIGH for 4 min, stirring every minute.
5 Beat in the egg, stir in the drained mixed vegetables and 25g (1oz) of the grated cheese.
6 Turn the mixture into the pastry case and sprinkle the remaining cheese on top.
7 Microwave on LOW for about 6 min or until the cheese has melted and the filling is thoroughly cooked.
8 Serve warm or cold.

Prawn scramble (serves 2)

15g ($\frac{1}{2}$oz) butter
4 eggs
4×15ml tbsp (4tbsp) milk
100g (4oz) peeled prawns
2 slices bread, toasted conventionally and buttered

1 Place the butter in an ovenproof bowl and microwave on HIGH for 30 sec.
2 Beat in the eggs and milk, mixing well together.
3 Microwave on HIGH for 2 min, stirring after 1 min and 1$\frac{1}{2}$ min.
4 Stir in prawns and continue cooking on HIGH for a further 1 min, or until egg mixture is cooked as preferred. Stir after 30 sec. Do not overcook.
5 Serve on hot buttered toast.

Fruits and desserts

Fresh or frozen fruit cooks to perfection in a microwave oven, and dried fruit, such as prunes, does not necessarily need to be soaked before cooking, although it does require time to rehydrate after the short cooking time. Whole fruits cooked in their skins, such as baked apples, should be pricked to prevent bursting during cooking. Frozen fruit can be defrosted in the oven, but should be removed when still slightly icy, and left to defrost completely during the standing time.

No need to steam puddings conventionally for hours; they can be cooked in just a few minutes in your microwave oven. Desserts which are to be served cold can be cooked in advance, when convenient, and often those to be served hot can be cooked while the main course is being eaten. Steamed and baked puddings with a cake-type topping should be removed from the oven when the top surface is still slightly moist, to prevent overcooking. This moisture will disappear during the standing time. Other desserts, such as crumbles, can be browned on top under a preheated conventional grill, if preferred. Double-crust pies should be baked conventionally because they require the dry heat of a conventional oven to retain their shape, as well as to crisp and brown the pastry.

Guide to defrosting 450g (1lb) frozen fruit

Fruit	Approx. Time on LOW Setting	Standing Time	Special Instructions
Apples, sliced	6–7 min	10 min, or until defrosted	Stir during defrosting
Apricots, halved and stoned	6–7 min	20 min, or until defrosted	Stir during defrosting
Blackberries and other soft berry fruits	4–5 min	10 min, or until defrosted	Shake during defrosting
Blackcurrants, redcurrants	6 min	10 min, or until defrosted	Stir during defrosting
Gooseberries	7–8 min	10 min, or until defrosted	Stir during defrosting
Peaches, whole	6–7 min	20 min, or until defrosted	Rearrange during defrosting
Plums, damsons, greengages	8 min	10 min, or until defrosted	Stir during defrosting
Rhubarb	8 min	10 min, or until defrosted	Shake during defrosting

Christmas pudding (page 101); Strawberry trifle (page 101); Rhubarb fool (page 100)

Guide to cooking fresh fruit

Fruit	Quantity	Approximate cooking time on HIGH setting	Standing time
Apples peeled, cored and sliced	450g (1lb)	4–5 min	2 min
baked	1 medium	2½–3 min	2 min
	2 medium	4–5 min	3 min
	4 medium	7–8 min	4 min
Apricots, halved and stoned	450g (1lb)	6–7 min	2 min
Blackberries and other soft berry fruits	450g (1lb)	3–4 min	2 min
Blackcurrants, redcurrants	450g (1lb)	3–4 min	2 min
Gooseberries	450g (1lb)	3–4 min	2 min
Peaches, halved and stoned	4	4–5min	2 min
Pears, skinned, halved and cored, sprinkled with lemon juice	450g (1lb)	7–8 min	3 min
Plums, damsons, greengages, stoned	450g (1lb)	4–5 min	2 min
Rhubarb, cut into 2.5cm (1in) lengths	450g (1lb)	7–8 min	3 min

Rhubarb fool *(serves 2–3)*

1 scant × 15ml tbsp (1tbsp) custard powder
15g (½oz) sugar
150ml (¼pt) milk
350g (12oz) prepared rhubarb, cut into 2.5cm (1in) lengths
4 × 15ml tbsp (4tbsp) orange juice
50g (2oz) sugar, or to taste
red food colouring, optional
whipped cream

1 Blend the custard powder and 15g (½oz) sugar with a little of the measured milk, in a Pyrex or suitable jug.
2 Gradually stir in remaining milk.
3 Microwave on HIGH for 2 min or until custard has boiled and thickened. Stir after 1 and 1½ min.
4 Set aside, to cool slightly.
5 Meanwhile place the rhubarb, orange juice and sugar in an ovenproof casserole.
6 Cover with a tight-fitting lid or plastic wrap and microwave on HIGH for 6 min, stirring after 3 min.
7 Purée the rhubarb with the custard in a blender, or sieve the rhubarb and beat into the custard.
8 Add a few drops of red food colouring, sparingly, if necessary.
9 Pour into individual serving dishes, cool and refrigerate.
10 Decorate with whipped cream.

Strawberry trifle *(serves 6)*

Cake base
50g (2oz) soft tub margarine
50g (2oz) caster sugar
50g (2oz) self-raising flour
pinch of salt
1 egg
2×5ml tsp (2tsp) warm water
Filling
strawberry jam, optional
1×425g (15oz) can strawberries
3×15ml tbsp (3tbsp) sherry
2×15ml tbsp (2tbsp) custard powder or
   strawberry flavoured blancmange powder
1½×15ml tbsp (1½tbsp) caster sugar
600ml (1pt) milk
To decorate
whipped cream
a few fresh strawberries, or glacé cherries and
angelica, or flaked almonds.

1 Place all the cake-base ingredients in a mixing bowl and beat together for 2 min by
   hand, or for 1 min if using an electric food
   mixer.
2 Turn the mixture into a greased 16.5cm
   (6½in) ovenproof flan dish, the base lined
   with greased greaseproof paper.
3 Microwave on HIGH for 2½ min or until
   cooked in the centre. Leave to stand 2 min.
   Turn out and leave until cold. Split and
   sandwich together with jam, if used.
4 Cut or break cake into pieces and place in
   the bottom of a glass serving dish.
5 Sprinkle with 2tbsp of the fruit juice and the
   sherry.
6 Arrange the drained strawberries on top
   and leave to soak.
7 Meanwhile, blend the custard or blancmange powder and sugar with a little of the
   milk in a large ovenproof jug or bowl. Stir in
   remaining milk.
8 Microwave on HIGH for 5½ min or until thickened. Stir every minute.
9 Cover with plastic wrap to prevent a skin
   forming, and leave to cool slightly.
10 Pour the custard over the fruit. Cool and
   refrigerate.

11 When completely cold decorate with whipped cream and fresh strawberries, glacé
   cherries and angelica, or flaked almonds.

VARIATIONS
1 Substitute 225g (8oz) fresh sliced strawberries for canned ones, reserving a few to
   decorate. Increase sherry to 4 tbsp.
2 Substitute other canned or fresh fruits, eg
   kiwi fruit.

Christmas pudding
(makes 2×900g/2lb puddings)

100g (4oz) plain flour
125g (5oz) breadcrumbs
1×5ml tsp (1tsp) mixed spice
150g (6oz) soft brown sugar
150g (6oz) shredded suet
50g (2oz) chopped mixed peel
550g (1¼lb) mixed dried fruit
1 lemon, grated rind and juice
1×100g (4oz) dessert apple, peeled and grated
3 eggs, beaten
120ml (4fl oz) milk
4×15ml tbsp (4tbsp) brandy or stout
2×15ml tbsp (2tbsp) black treacle

1 Combine all the dry ingredients in a large
   mixing bowl.
2 Add the remaining ingredients and mix well.
3 Divide the mixture between 2×1 litre (1¾pt)
   ovenproof pudding basins which have been
   well greased or lined with plastic wrap.
4 Cover with plastic wrap.
5 Cook each pudding separately. Microwave
   on HIGH for 5 min, leave to stand for 4 min.
   Cook on HIGH for a further 5 min, then leave
   to stand for at least 5 min before turning out.
6 Cook the second pudding in the same way.

Note: *The puddings can be made in advance
and stored, wrapped in greaseproof paper and
aluminium foil, in the refrigerator. When
required, remove wrappings and place pudding
on a serving plate or dish and cover with plastic
wrap. Reheat each pudding on HIGH for about
2½ min or until just warm to the touch. Do not
overheat. A single portion will reheat in
45–60 sec on HIGH, depending on portion size.*

Chocolate fondue *(serves 4–6)*

225g (8oz) plain chocolate or chocolate
   flavoured cake covering
150ml ($\frac{1}{4}$pt) double cream
2×15ml tbsp (2tbsp) rum or brandy
For serving
pink and white marshmallows
a selection of fresh or drained canned fruit,
   sliced or cut into bite-sized pieces
cubes of sponge cake

1 Break the chocolate or cake covering into
   small pieces and place in a non-metallic fondue pot or medium-sized flameproof casserole.
2 Add 4tbsp of cream.
3 Microwave on HIGH for 2 min or until chocolate has melted. Stir after 1 min and 1$\frac{1}{2}$ min.
4 Stir in the rum or brandy.
5 Swirl in the remaining cream to give a mar-
   bled effect.
6 Keep warm over a fondue burner or spirit
   lamp.
7 Serve with marshmallows, fruit and sponge
   cake to spear onto fondue forks and dip into
   the fondue.

Chocolate mousse flan *(serves 6)*

75g (3oz) butter, cut into pieces
150g (6oz) digestive biscuits, crushed
125g (5oz) plain chocolate or chocolate
   flavoured cake covering
3 eggs, separated
2×15ml tbsp (2tbsp) rum, optional
150ml ($\frac{1}{4}$pt) double or whipping cream
grated chocolate or 1 flake bar, crumbled

1 Place the butter in an ovenproof 17.5cm
   (7in) flan dish and microwave on HIGH for
   1$\frac{1}{4}$ min or until melted.
2 Stir in the biscuit crumbs and bind together.
3 Press the crumb mixture over the base and
   sides of the dish.
4 Microwave on HIGH for 1$\frac{1}{2}$ min, to set the
   crust. Leave to cool.
5 Break the chocolate or cake covering into
   small pieces in a medium-sized, ovenproof
   bowl.

6 Microwave on HIGH for 1$\frac{3}{4}$ min or until
   melted, stirring after 1 min and 1$\frac{1}{2}$ min.
7 Beat in the egg yolks and rum, if used.
8 In a separate bowl whisk the egg whites
   until stiff, then fold them into the chocolate
   mixture.
9 Turn the mixture into the flan case. Cool
   and refrigerate until set.
10 Decorate with whipped cream and sprinkle
   the chocolate on top.

Cherries jubilee *(serves 4)*

1×425g (15oz) can stoned black cherries in
   syrup
pinch of ground cinnamon
sugar, only if necessary
2×5ml tsp (2tsp) arrowroot
60ml (2fl oz) Cognac
vanilla ice-cream

1 Drain the cherries; measure the juice and
   make up to 300ml ($\frac{1}{2}$pt) with water if necessary. Stir in cinnamon and sugar (if juice is
   too sour).
2 Blend the arrowroot to a smooth paste with a
   little of the measured juice in a large Pyrex or
   ovenproof jug.
3 Stir in remaining juice and microwave on
   HIGH for 3$\frac{1}{2}$ min or until sauce has boiled and
   thickened. Stir every minute.
4 Stir in the cherries and heat on HIGH for a
   further 30 sec.
5 Pour the cherry sauce into a flameproof dish.
6 Measure the Cognac into a small Pyrex jug
   and warm on HIGH for 15 sec.
7 Pour over the cherries at the serving table and
   ignite.
8 Serve as soon as the flames have died away,
   over scoops of vanilla ice-cream.

*Chocolate fondue (above); Individual egg custards
(page 104)*

Apple and blackberry crumble *(serves 4)*

450g (1lb) cooking apples, peeled, cored and
thinly sliced
225g (8oz) blackberries, fresh or defrosted if
frozen
75g (3oz) soft brown sugar
75g (3oz) butter
150g (6oz) plain flour
75g (3oz) demerara sugar

1 Place alternate layers of apples, blackberries
and soft brown sugar in a greased 1.1 litre
(2pt) flameproof pie dish.
2 Cover and microwave on HIGH for 5 min.
3 Meanwhile rub the butter into the flour until
the mixture resembles fine breadcrumbs. Stir
in 50g (2oz) of the demerara sugar.
4 Uncover the pie dish and spread the softened
fruit in an even layer.
5 Sprinkle the crumble mixture over the fruit
and top with the remaining 25g (1oz) of
demerara sugar.
6 Microwave, uncovered, on HIGH for 7 min.
7 Brown under a conventional grill, preheated
on a medium setting.
8 Serve hot or cold with custard, cream or ice-
cream.

Alternative Recipe
Quick crumble: for a really quick dessert, melt
40g (1½oz) butter in an ovenproof bowl for
1 min. Using a fork, stir in 100g (4oz) crushed
digestive biscuits until thoroughly coated in butter. Turn out onto a flat surface to cool. Meanwhile turn the contents of a 385g (13.6oz) can
apple and blackberry pie filling into an ovenproof pie dish. Cover and heat on HIGH for
2½ min. Uncover, sprinkle the crumbed biscuits
on top and microwave on HIGH for 2 min. Stand
5 min before serving hot. Can be served cold.

Individual egg custards *(serves 4)*

450ml (¾pt) milk
3 eggs, lightly beaten
25g (1oz) caster sugar
a few drops of vanilla essence
grated or ground nutmeg

1 Place milk in an ovenproof jug and microwave on HIGH for 2½ min or until it just begins
to bubble around the outside. Do not allow to
boil.
2 Add the eggs, sugar and essence. Whisk
lightly to combine ingredients.
3 Strain the custard and divide equally among
4 individual ovenproof dishes or ramekins.
Sprinkle with nutmeg.
4 Arrange the dishes in a circle in the oven.
5 Microwave on LOW for 15 min or until just
set. Remove the custards individually if you
find that in your oven they are cooking at
different rates. Do not overcook or custard
will curdle.
6 Leave to cool. Refrigerate and serve chilled.

Fruit suet pudding *(serves 4–5)*

Suet pastry
100g (4oz) self-raising flour
50g (2oz) breadcrumbs
75g (3oz) shredded suet
25g (1oz) caster sugar
cold water to mix
Filling
350g (12oz) prepared fruit, e.g. sliced apples,
rhubarb, berry fruits or 1×385g (13.6oz) can
pie filling
50–75g (2–3oz) sugar or to taste, if using fresh
fruit

1 To make pastry, mix together the dry ingredients and add enough water to give a light
elastic dough.
2 Roll out two-thirds of the pastry and line a
greased 900ml (1½pt) ovenproof pudding
bowl.
3 Place the filling in the pastry-lined bowl.
4 Roll out remaining pastry to make a lid. Wet
the edge with water and press the lid firmly in
place, sealing the pastry edges well together.
5 Cover loosely with greased greaseproof
paper and microwave on HIGH for about
8 min.
6 Stand for 2–3 min before serving from the
bowl, or carefully turning out onto a heated
serving dish.

Fruited steamed pudding *(serves 3–4)*

50g (2oz) soft tub margarine
50g (2oz) caster sugar
50g (2oz) self-raising flour
pinch of salt
1 egg
25g (1oz) raisins or sultanas
25g (1oz) currants
2×5ml tsp (2tsp) warm water

1 Place the margarine, sugar, flour, salt and egg in a mixing bowl and mix well together for 2 min by hand, or for 1 min using an electric food mixer.
2 Stir in the fruit and water.
3 Turn the mixture into a greased 900ml (1½pt) ovenproof pudding basin which has been base-lined with a circle of greased grease-proof paper.
4 Microwave on HIGH for 3 min or until surface is just slightly moist and pudding is cooked in the centre.
5 Leave to stand for 2–3 min before turning out to serve.

VARIATIONS
Jam cap pudding: grease but do not line the base of the basin. Spoon in 2tbsp jam. Make up pudding mixture as given above, omitting dried fruit. Spread mixture on top of jam and cook on HIGH for 3½ min or until cooked in the centre.
Syrup sponge: proceed as for Jam Cap pudding, substituting 2tbsp golden syrup for jam.
Large family pudding: double the quantity of ingredients and place the mixture in a greased 1.1 litre (2pt) pudding basin. Cook on HIGH for 5 min or until cooked in centre.

Saucy sponge *(serves 4)*

1 packet Saucy Sponge mix

1 Empty the sponge mix into an ovenproof 15cm (6in) base diameter soufflé dish.
2 Add egg, water and sauce mix as instructed on the packet.
3 Microwave on HIGH for 4½ min or until sponge is cooked when tested in the centre with a fine skewer or wooden cocktail stick.

4 If necessary, return to the oven for about a further 30 sec.
5 Leave to stand 5 min before serving straight from the dish.

Note: *During cooking the sponge rises, leaving the sauce in the bottom of the dish.*

Creamy rice pudding *(serves 4)*

240ml (8fl oz) evaporated milk
360ml (12fl oz) water
50g (2oz) short-grain rice
25g (1oz) caster sugar
ground nutmeg, optional

1 Mix the milk with the water and pour into a buttered 2.8 litre (5pt) ovenproof bowl.
2 Stir in the rice and sugar and cover with plastic wrap.
3 Microwave on HIGH for 8 min or until boiling. Stir twice.
4 Reduce setting to LOW and continue cooking for about a further 45 min or until the rice is soft and the mixture is creamy. Stir at least 3 times during cooking.
5 Leave to stand, covered, for 10 min before serving sprinkled with nutmeg, if used. Alternatively serve cold.

VARIATIONS
1 Stir in 50g (2oz) raisins or sultanas for the final 10 min cooking time.
2 For a less rich, less creamy pudding, use 600ml (1pt) fresh milk instead of evaporated milk and water. Proceed as above.
3 After cooking the rice pudding as given above, using either 600ml (1pt) fresh milk or evaporated milk and water, turn it into a shallow flameproof dish, sprinkle with demerara sugar and place under a pre-heated conventional grill until the sugar has caramelized.

Fruit flan *(serves 5–6)*

Shortcrust pastry
125g (5oz) plain flour
pinch of salt
75g (3oz) butter or margarine
1 egg yolk, beaten
a few drops of yellow food colouring, optional
1–2×15ml tbsp (1–2tbsp) water
Filling
1×397g (14oz) can pie filling
150ml ($\frac{1}{4}$pt) double or whipping cream

1 Sieve the flour and salt into a bowl. Rub the fat into the flour until mixture resembles fine breadcrumbs.
2 Stir in egg yolk. Add the yellow food colouring, if used, to the water. Stir in enough water to bind the pastry together.
3 Roll the pastry out into a 22.5cm (9in) round and line a 17.5cm (7in) ovenproof flan dish. Ease the pastry into the dish without stretching, and press down well onto the base and sides of the dish, excluding air. Leave the pastry about 0.6cm ($\frac{1}{4}$in) above the rim of the dish.
4 Place a piece of kitchen paper over the pastry base and lay a slightly smaller ovenproof plate or dish on top of the paper.
5 Microwave on HIGH for 4 min
6 Remove the retaining plate or dish and kitchen paper. Microwave on HIGH for 1 min longer or until pastry is almost dry. Leave until cold.
7 Meanwhile turn the pie filling into an ovenproof bowl. Cover and microwave on HIGH for 2 min. Leave to cool slightly.
8 Pour into flan case, cool and refrigerate.
9 Decorate with whipped cream before serving.

VARIATION
Substitute fresh or drained canned fruit for pie filling and arrange in flan case. Heat 3tbsp redcurrant jelly with 1tbsp of water on HIGH for 45 sec or until melted. Pour jelly over fruit when it begins to thicken. Leave to cool and decorate with whipped cream.

Brandied raspberries *(serves 2–3)*

1×411g (14$\frac{1}{2}$oz) can raspberries in syrup
3×5ml tsp (3 level tsp) arrowroot
1×15ml tbsp (1tbsp) brandy
150ml ($\frac{1}{4}$pt) whipping cream, whipped
grated nutmeg, optional

1 Drain the raspberries, reserving the juice.
2 Blend the juice and arrowroot together in a Pyrex measuring jug.
3 Microwave on HIGH for about 2$\frac{1}{2}$ min or until the sauce has boiled and thickened. Stir every minute.
4 Fold in the brandy and raspberries.
5 Pour into individual serving dishes or stemmed glasses. Cool and refrigerate until set.
6 Decorate with whipped cream and sprinkle with nutmeg before serving with boudoir biscuits or shortbread fingers.

Apple and date meringue *(serves 3–4)*

450g (1lb) prepared weight, peeled, cored and sliced cooking apples
50g (2oz) dates, chopped
sugar to taste
2 eggs, separated
good pinch of cornflour
good pinch of cream of tartar
4×15ml tbsp (4tbsp) caster sugar

1 Place apples and dates in an ovenproof dish. Cover and cook on HIGH for 6–8 min or until the apples are soft.
2 Beat to a purée, add sugar to taste and stir in egg yolks.
3 Turn the mixture into an ovenproof pie dish.
4 Whisk the egg whites, cornflour and cream of tartar until standing in soft peaks.
5 Add sugar a tablespoon at a time and beat until stiff.
6 Spoon the meringue mixture over the apple and date mixture and fork or fluff up in peaks.
7 Microwave on LOW for about 6 min or until the meringue is set.
8 Brown under a pre-heated conventional grill for 2–4 min if preferred.
9 Serve hot or cold.

Bread, cakes, scones and biscuits

Generally speaking, yeast doughs are best proved and baked conventionally, although if a loaf is required in a hurry a packet bread mix gives an acceptable result, especially if the top, sides and base of the loaf are crisped and browned under a preheated conventional grill at the end of the short microwave cooking period. Bread and bread products can be quickly defrosted or reheated in the oven and should be placed on kitchen paper to absorb moisture. Do not overheat bread or it will become tough, dry and hard.

Cakes cook quickly in the oven and usually rise more than when baked conventionally. They should be removed from the oven when they are still slightly moist on top. The moisture will disappear during the standing time. Do not overcook cakes, or they will be dry and hard when they cool. Do not fill containers more than one-third to one-half full. While most cakes are cooked on HIGH setting, rich fruit cakes benefit from longer slower cooking on LOW setting. Do not flour cake containers. For easy removal it is advisable to line the base with greased greaseproof paper, as well as grease the container. Cakes cooked in a microwave oven are very light in texture, so if they are to be iced or filled they are easier to handle if, after cooling, they are refrigerated for about half an hour.

Scones are best cooked in a microwave browning dish. Otherwise bake them conventionally.

Biscuits are really best baked conventionally, so apart from flapjacks, muesli bars and millionaire's shortbread they are omitted from this book.

Bread mix loaf *(makes 1 loaf)*

1×283g (10oz) packet white or brown bread mix

1 Make up the bread mix according to packet instructions.
2 Place in a 22.5×12.5×7.5cm (9×5×3in) microwave loaf dish.
3 Leave to prove as instructed on packet.
4 Microwave on HIGH for 5½ min or until bread sounds hollow when turned out and tapped on the base.
5 Remove the loaf from the dish and brown all sides under a preheated conventional grill.

Wholewheat soda bread *(makes 8 wedges)*

275g (10oz) plain wholewheat flour
1×5ml tsp (1tsp) salt
1×5ml tsp (1tsp) bicarbonate of soda
2×5ml tsp (2tsp) cream of tartar
25g (1oz) margarine
180ml (6floz) milk, approximately
nibbed wheat or rolled oats

1 Place the first four ingredients in a mixing bowl and rub in the margarine until mixture resembles fine breadcrumbs.
2 Add enough milk to give a soft dough.
3 Knead the dough lightly and roll out into a 20cm (8in) round.
4 Place on lightly floured greaseproof paper on a plate without metal trim.

5 Score the dough deeply into 8 wedges. Sprinkle with nibbed wheat or rolled oats.
6 Microwave on HIGH for 5 min or until cooked through to the centre.
7 Leave to stand for about 10 min.
8 Serve warm. Best eaten fresh.

Note: *After step 6 above, the loaf can be transferred to a grill rack and be browned on the top and base under a preheated conventional grill.*

VARIATION
Add 50g (2oz) raisins and 25g (1oz) caster sugar to the mixture after step 1. Proceed as given above.

Treacle scones *(makes 8)*

40g (1½oz) margarine
225g (8oz) self-raising wholewheat flour
pinch of salt
1×15ml tbsp (1tbsp) soft brown sugar
1×5ml tsp (1tsp) baking powder
1×15ml tbsp (1tbsp) black treacle
1 egg, beaten
50ml (2fl oz) milk or milk and water mixed

1 Rub margarine into flour and salt until mixture resembles fine breadcrumbs.
2 Stir in sugar and baking powder.
3 Mix the treacle with the beaten egg and milk or milk and water.
4 Stir the liquid into the dry ingredients.
5 Turn the mixture onto a floured surface, knead lightly and shape into a large round 1.25cm (½in) thick.
6 Cut into 8 triangles.
7 Preheat a microwave browning dish according to manufacturer's instructions. Time will depend on size of dish used.
8 Grease the base of the preheated dish lightly with oil.
9 Arrange the scones in the dish with the narrow, pointed ends towards the centre.
10 Microwave on HIGH for 2 min.
11 Turn scones over and microwave on HIGH for about a further 2 min.
12 Serve hot or cold, split and buttered.

Wholemeal scone-based pizza *(serves 2–3)*

25g (1oz) margarine
100g (4oz) wholemeal self-raising flour
½×5ml tsp (½tsp) baking powder
pinch of salt
1 egg, beaten
milk to mix
1×227g (8oz) can tomatoes, drained and chopped
1 small onion, grated
pinch of oregano or 1×5ml tsp (1tsp) pizza seasoning
pepper
75g (3oz) grated cheese, preferably mozzarella
1×50g (1¾oz) can anchovies, drained
black olives or sliced green stuffed olives

1 Rub margarine into flour until mixture resembles fine breadcrumbs. Stir in baking powder and salt.
2 Add egg and enough milk to give a soft dough.
3 Knead lightly and roll out into a 20cm (8in) round.
4 Place on a piece of non-stick baking parchment on a plate without metal trim.
5 Microwave on HIGH for 2½ min.
6 Mix the tomatoes and onion together and spread on the base.
7 Sprinkle with oregano or pizza seasoning, and pepper.
8 Top with grated cheese, the anchovy fillets which have been cut in half lengthways, and the olives.
9 Microwave on HIGH for 3–3½ min or until cooked through.
10 Remove parchment before serving.

Queen cakes *(makes about 18)*

100g (4oz) soft tub margarine
100g (4oz) caster sugar
100g (4oz) self-raising flour
pinch of salt
2 eggs, beaten
50g (2oz) currants
2×15ml tbsp (2tbsp) warm water
yellow food colouring, optional

1 Place all the ingredients in a mixing bowl. Mix well together for about 2 min by hand, or 1 min with an electric food mixer.
2 Half-fill 6 double-thickness paper cake cases, using about one third of the cake mixture.
3 Place these either in a 6-ring microwave muffin pan, or in 6 ovenproof cups without metal trim.
4 If using ovenproof cups, arrange them in a circle in the oven.
5 Microwave the 6 cakes on HIGH for 2 min or until cooked. Check after $1\frac{1}{2}$ min and re-arrange the cups if necessary for more even cooking.
6 Transfer the cooked cakes to a cooling rack and cook the remaining mixture in the same way.

VARIATIONS
1 Substitute sultanas or chocolate chips for the currants.
2 Use wholewheat self-raising flour instead of white, and substitute chopped dates for the currants.

Chocolate fruit crunch (makes 8–10 wedges)

225g (8oz) digestive biscuits, broken into small pieces
50g (2oz) raisins
50g (2oz) glacé cherries, chopped
100g (4oz) plain chocolate flavoured cake covering
100g (4oz) butter, cut into small pieces
2 × 15ml tbsp (2tbsp) golden syrup
Topping
100g (4oz) plain chocolate flavoured cake covering
25g (1oz) flaked blanched almonds, optional

1 Place the biscuits, raisins and cherries in a mixing bowl.
2 Break the cake covering into small pieces and place in an ovenproof glass bowl (not lead crystal) with the butter and syrup.
3 Microwave on HIGH for 2 min or until the cake covering and butter have melted. Stir after 1 min.

4 Add this melted mixture to the dry ingredients, stirring well until thoroughly coated.
5 Press the mixture into a 20cm (8in) plain flan ring placed on a flat serving plate.
6 Chill in the refrigerator for at least 1 hr.
7 Break the cake covering for the topping into small pieces and place in a small ovenproof glass bowl (not lead crystal).
8 Microwave on HIGH for $1\frac{1}{2}$ min or until melted, stirring after 1 min. Do not over-heat.
9 Spread evenly over the cake and either sprinkle with flaked almonds, or mark with a fork, to decorate.
10 Leave topping to set before serving.

Chocolate rum truffles (makes 12)

50g (2oz) butter
6 × 15ml tbsp (6tbsp) desiccated coconut
3 × 15ml tbsp (3tbsp) porridge oats
3 × 15ml tbsp (3tbsp) caster or sieved icing sugar
2 × 15ml tbsp (2tbsp) sieved cocoa
1 × 15ml tbsp (1tbsp) rum
desiccated coconut or chocolate vermicelli for coating

1 Place the butter in a medium-sized Pyrex or ovenproof bowl and microwave on HIGH for $1\frac{1}{2}$ min or until melted.
2 Stir in the dry ingredients and mix all well together.
3 Stir in the rum.
4 Take heaped teaspoons of the mixture and form into small balls.
5 Roll in desiccated coconut or chocolate vermicelli.
6 Chill in refrigerator and serve in paper sweet cases.

VARIATION
Surprise truffles: with wet hands, mould the truffle mixture round marshmallows. Roll in desiccated coconut or chocolate vermicelli. Chill and serve in paper cake cases.

Rich fruit cake *(makes one 20cm/8in cake)*

2 eggs, beaten
100g (4oz) dark soft brown sugar
2×15ml tbsp (2tbsp) black treacle
scant 75ml (3fl oz) vegetable oil
150g (6oz) self-raising flour
1×5ml tsp (1tsp) mixed spice
good pinch of salt
120ml (4fl oz) milk
450g (1lb) mixed dried fruit
100g (4oz) raisins
50g (2oz) glacé cherries, quartered
100g (4oz) chopped nuts or flaked blanched
   almonds, optional

1 Place the eggs, sugar and treacle in a large mixing bowl and mix well together. Beat in the oil.
2 Sieve the flour and spice together and stir in salt.
3 Stir the dry ingredients into the egg mixture alternately with the milk. Mix well together but do not beat.
4 Stir in the fruit and nuts, if used.
5 Place the mixture in a 20cm (8in) round deep straight-sided ovenproof dish, such as a soufflé dish, which has been greased and lined with greased greaseproof paper.
6 Press the mixture into the dish and level the top.
7 Microwave on LOW for 45 min, then test for readiness by inserting a fine skewer in the centre. The cake should be cooked in the centre although the top surface may be slightly moist. If necessary return the cake to the oven for a further few minutes.
8 Leave until almost cold before turning cake out of dish.

Note:

1 *This cake is ideal to serve as a Christmas cake. When the cake is cold, skewer with brandy and store wrapped in greaseproof paper and foil for about a week to mature. Cover with marzipan and royal icing in the usual way.*
2 *If, with your oven, you experience difficulty in cooking the centre or centre base of deep cakes without overcooking the outside edges, place the cake dish on an upturned ovenproof plate, without metal trim, and cook as given above.*

Chocolate cup cakes *(makes 12–16)*

50g (2oz) margarine
50g (2oz) dark soft brown sugar
1 egg, beaten
few drops of vanilla essence
75g (3oz) self-raising flour, sieved
25g (1oz) cocoa, sieved
3–4×15ml tbsp (3–4tbsp) milk
75g (3oz) plain chocolate flavoured cake
   covering
chopped nuts or walnut pieces, optional

1 Cream margarine and sugar together until light and fluffy.
2 Beat in egg and vanilla essence.
3 Fold in the flour and cocoa evenly, then gently stir in enough milk to give a very soft mixture.
4 Half fill 6 double-thickness paper cake cases with some of the mixture.
5 Place these either in a 6-ring microwave muffin pan, or in 6 ovenproof cups without metal trim.
6 If using ovenproof cups, arrange them in a circle in the oven.
7 Cook the 6 cakes on HIGH for 1½–2 min. Check after 1 min and rearrange the cups if necessary for more even cooking.
8 Transfer the cooked cakes to a cooling rack and cook the remaining mixture in the same way.
9 When the cakes are cold, break the cake covering into a small Pyrex bowl and melt on HIGH for about 1 min. Stir after 30 sec, and after melting.
10 Dip the tops of the cakes first in the melted mixture and then in chopped nuts, if used. Alternatively, place a walnut piece in the centre of each cake after coating top with chocolate.

Rich fruit cake (above); Madeleines (page 112); Chocolate cup cakes (above); Surprise truffles (page 109)

Madeleines *(makes 10 small cakes)*

100g (4oz) soft tub margarine
100g (4oz) caster sugar
100g (4oz) self-raising flour
pinch of salt
2 eggs
1 × 15ml tbsp (1tbsp) warm water
5 × 15ml tbsp (5tbsp) red jam
desiccated coconut
5 glacé cherries, halved
small pieces of angelica, optional

1 Place the margarine, sugar, flour, salt, eggs and water in a mixing bowl. Mix well together for about 2 min by hand, or 1 min with an electric food mixer.
2 Lightly grease a 6-way microwave muffin pan or the insides of 5 microwave mini dishes.
3 Divide half the cake mixture among 5 of the muffin pans or mini dishes.
4 Place the muffin pan, or the mini dishes arranged in a circle, in the oven.
5 Microwave on HIGH for about 2 min. Re-arrange the mini dishes after 1 min. Some of the cakes may cook before others; remove as necessary.
6 Leave cakes to stand for a few minutes before turning out to cool.
7 Cook the remaining half of the cake mixture in the same way.
8 Place the jam in a Pyrex or ovenproof bowl and heat on HIGH for 45–60 sec, stirring after 30 sec.
9 Brush the cold cakes with the jam, and roll in coconut. Decorate with halved glacé cherries and angelica if used.

Note: *To make 5 large madeleines, divide the mixture equally among five paper drinking cups. Arrange in a circle in the oven and microwave on HIGH for about 3½ min, rearranging the cups after 1½ min and removing any which cook more quickly than others. Finish as given above.*

Fluffy meringues
(makes about 30 small meringues)

½ an egg white
150g (6oz) sieved icing sugar, approximately

1 Place the ½ egg white in a mixing bowl.
2 Using a fork, mix in enough icing sugar to give a stiff mixture which can be rolled between the palms of the hand.
3 Roll the mixture into small balls the size of a marble.
4 Arrange the balls, 4 at a time, well apart in a circle on kitchen paper on a large flat round ovenproof plate, without metal trim.
5 Microwave on HIGH for about 1¼ min, during which time the meringues will increase dramatically in size.
6 Transfer to a cooling rack and repeat with remaining mixture, starting with a cold plate and fresh kitchen paper each time.
7 Serve with ice-cream or fruit, or sandwich together with whipped cream.

VARIATIONS
Sprinkle instant coffee powder onto the mixture before cooking or add a few drops of food colouring – and corresponding food flavouring – to the mixture.

Crispy clusters *(makes 10)*

100g (4oz) milk or plain chocolate flavoured cake covering
25g (1oz) Rice Crispies
1 × 15ml tbsp (1tbsp) raisins or chopped dates, optional

1 Break the cake covering into small pieces into an ovenproof glass bowl (not lead crystal).
2 Microwave on HIGH for 1½ min or until melted, stirring after 1 min. Do not overheat.
3 Stir in the Rice Crispies and raisins or dates, if used. Mix all well together until thoroughly coated.
4 Using two forks, place the mixture in small heaps on waxed or non-stick paper.
5 Leave to set before serving.

American walnut squares *(makes 16)*

2 eggs
225g (8oz) caster sugar
½×5ml tsp (½tsp) vanilla essence
125g (5oz) butter or block margarine
100g (4oz) self-raising flour, sieved
50g (2oz) cocoa
50–100g (2–4oz) walnuts, chopped

1 Beat the eggs, sugar and essence together in a mixing bowl until creamy.
2 Cut up the butter or margarine, place in a Pyrex jug and microwave on HIGH for 1 min or until melted.
3 Add the melted fat to the egg and sugar mixture.
4 Fold in the sieved flour and cocoa. Stir in the walnuts.
5 Turn the mixture into a non-metallic 20cm (8in) square dish, greased and base-lined with greased greaseproof paper. Level the surface.
6 Microwave on HIGH for 9 min or until the top surface is only slightly moist. Check for readiness at 8 min.
7 Leave to cool in the dish. When cold, cut into squares.

Note:

1 *To prevent overcooking the outside edges (especially at the corners) before the centre of the cake is cooked, it may be necessary to protect these areas by shielding them with small pieces of smooth aluminium foil attached to the top of the dish towards the end of the cooking time. Do not allow aluminium foil to touch any part of the oven interior.*
2 *The walnut squares can be coated with melted chocolate after cooling. To do this break up 100g (4oz) chocolate into a small Pyrex bowl and microwave on HIGH for about 1½ min. Stir after 1 min.*

Wholewheat date cake

100g (4oz) margarine
225g (8oz) self-raising wholewheat flour
100g (4oz) dark soft brown sugar
150g (6oz) dates, chopped
2 eggs, beaten
5×15ml tbsp (5tbsp) milk, approximately

1 Grease a 1.1 litre (2pt) Pyrex or ovenproof straight-sided soufflé dish and base line with greased greaseproof paper.
2 Rub the margarine into the flour until mixture resembles fine breadcrumbs.
3 Stir in the sugar and dates.
4 Stir in the beaten eggs and enough milk to give a softish batter.
5 Spoon the mixture evenly into the prepared dish and leave to stand for 2–3 min.
6 Microwave on HIGH for 6¼–6½ min.
7 Leave to stand for 10 min before turning out.
8 Remove greaseproof paper from base and leave to cool.

Muesli bars *(makes 18)*

150g (6oz) milk or plain chocolate flavoured cake covering
3×15ml tbsp (3tbsp) golden syrup
25g (1oz) butter
225g (8oz) muesli with fruit and nuts
100g (4oz) milk or plain chocolate flavoured cake covering, optional

1 Break the 150g (6oz) cake covering into small pieces and place in an ovenproof glass bowl (not lead crystal) with the syrup and butter.
2 Microwave on HIGH for 2 min or until melted. Stir after 1 and 1½ min.
3 Stir in the muesli and mix well until evenly coated.
4 Press mixture evenly into a lightly greased 18.75cm (7½in) square tin.
5 Break the remaining 100g (4oz) cake covering, if used, into small pieces and melt as above on HIGH for about 1½ min. Stir after 1 min.
6 Spread over the mixture in the tin, mark with a fork to decorate, and refrigerate till set.
7 Cut into fingers.

Fruit scones *(makes 8–10)*

40g (1½oz) margarine
225g (8oz) self-raising flour
pinch of salt
1×15ml tbsp (1tbsp) caster sugar
1×5ml tsp (1tsp) baking powder
2×15ml tbsp (2tbsp) dried fruit (currants,
  raisins, sultanas)
1×15ml tbsp (1tbsp) golden syrup
1 egg, beaten
50ml (2fl oz) milk or milk and water mixed

1 Rub margarine into flour and salt until mixture resembles fine breadcrumbs.
2 Stir in sugar, baking powder and dried fruit.
3 Mix the syrup with the beaten egg and milk or milk and water.
4 Stir the liquid into the dry ingredients.
5 Turn the scone mixture onto a floured surface, knead lightly, and shape into a large round 1.25cm (½in) thick.
6 Cut into 8 triangles or into 5cm (2in) rounds.
7 Preheat a microwave browning dish according to manufacturer's instructions. Time will depend on size of dish used.
8 Grease the base of the preheated dish lightly with oil.
9 Place the scones in the dish with the narrow, pointed ends of triangles towards the centre.
10 Microwave on HIGH for 2 min.
11 Turn scones over and continue cooking on HIGH for about a further 2 min.
12 Serve hot or cold, split and buttered or spread with jam topped with cream.

Millionaire's shortbread *(makes 16 squares)*

Shortbread base
100g (4oz) butter
50g (2oz) caster sugar
50g (2oz) plain flour
50g (2oz) plain wholewheat or wholemeal flour
50g (2oz) ground rice
Filling
100g (4oz) margarine
1 small can sweetened condensed milk
4×15ml tbsp (4tbsp) golden syrup

100g (4oz) caster sugar
Topping
125g (5oz) plain chocolate flavoured cake
  covering.

1 Make the shortbread base. Cream butter and sugar together until very light and creamy.
2 Gradually work in the flours and ground rice. Knead lightly.
3 Press the mixture evenly into a 20–22.5cm (8–9in) square ovenproof dish which has been greased and lined with greased greaseproof paper extending slightly over the sides of the dish for easy removal of the cooked shortbread.
4 Cook the shortbread on HIGH for 4 min or until cooked in the centre.
5 Leave to stand and cool in the dish.
6 Meanwhile prepare the filling. Place the margarine, milk, syrup and sugar in a large 2.8 litre (5pt) ovenproof bowl.
7 Microwave on HIGH for 4 min, stirring every minute.
8 Continue cooking on HIGH, allowing the mixture to boil for 5 min or until caramel in colour and thickened. Stir at least every minute.
9 Beat the thickened mixture for 2–3 min until it is a pale fawn colour.
10 Pour onto shortbread base and leave to cool.
11 Break the cake covering into small pieces into an ovenproof bowl.
12 Microwave on HIGH for 1¾ min or until melted. Stir after 1 min and 1½ min.
13 Spread over the caramel filling and mark with a fork to decorate.
14 Leave to set before cutting into squares.

VARIATION
Use 100g (4oz) plain white flour and omit the 50g (2oz) plain wholewheat or wholemeal flour.

Flapjacks *(makes 12 fingers)*

4×15ml tbsp (4tbsp) golden syrup
75g (3oz) butter
75g (3oz) demerara sugar
150g (6oz) rolled oats
½×5ml tsp (½tsp) ground ginger, optional

1 Place the syrup, butter and sugar in an oven-proof glass bowl (not lead crystal).
2 Microwave on HIGH for 1½ min. Stir well to blend and dissolve sugar.
3 Stir in the rolled oats, and ginger if used, mixing all well together.
4 Turn the mixture into a lightly greased 20cm (8in) non-metallic square shallow dish, and spread evenly.
5 Microwave on HIGH for 3½ min or until set.
6 Mark into fingers while hot. Cut and serve when cold.

Note: *These are best eaten fresh since they will tend to soften even when stored in an airtight container.*

Victoria sandwich
(makes one 18.75–20cm/7½–8in cake)

150g (6oz) soft tub margarine
150g (6oz) caster sugar
150g (6oz) self-raising flour
pinch of salt
3 eggs
2×15ml tbsp (2tbsp) warm water
a few drops of yellow food colouring, optional
vanilla essence, optional

1 Place all the ingredients in a mixing bowl and mix all well together for about 2 min by hand, or 1 min with an electric food mixer.
2 Turn the mixture into a lightly greased oven-proof straight-sided 18.75–20cm (7½–8in) round deep dish which has been base-lined with greased greaseproof paper. Alternatively the dish can be lined with plastic wrap.
3 Level the top of the cake and microwave on HIGH for 5½ min. Test the centre of the cake for readiness with a fine skewer. If necessary return to the oven and cook for about another 30–60 sec. The top of the cake may still be slightly moist, even though the centre is cooked.
4 Leave cake to stand until almost cold before turning out to finish cooling. During this time the top surface will dry.
5 When cold, refrigerate for about 30 min to make cutting easier.

6 Cut cake in half horizontally and spread with jam, cream, or buttercream.
7 Sprinkle top of cake with caster or sieved icing sugar. Alternatively ice, or decorate it with cream.

Note: *If you experience difficulty with your oven in cooking the centre or centre base of the cake without overcooking the outside edges, place the cake dish on an upturned ovenproof plate, without metal trim, and cook as given above.*

Victoria sandwich layers
(makes two 16.5cm/6½in layers)

100g (4oz) soft tub margarine
100g (4oz) caster sugar
100g (4oz) self-raising flour
pinch of salt
2 eggs
1½×15ml tbsp (1½tbsp) warm water
a few drops of lemon food colouring, optional
vanilla essence, optional

1 Place all the ingredients in a mixing bowl and mix well together for about 2 min by hand, or 1 min with an electric food mixer.
2 Divide the mixture equally between two lightly greased shallow ovenproof 16.25cm (6½in) round flan dishes, base-lined with greased greaseproof paper.
3 Place one layer in the oven and microwave on LOW for about 4½ min. Test the centre for readiness with a fine skewer or wooden cock-tail stick. If necessary cook for about a further 30–60 sec. The top surface may still be slightly moist even though the centre is cooked.
4 Leave to stand until almost cold before turning out of dish.
5 Cook the second layer in the same way.
6 When the layers are cold, sandwich together with jam, cream or buttercream. Sprinkle top with caster or sieved icing sugar. Alternatively ice, or decorate it with cream.

VARIATION
Chocolate sponge layers: substitute 25g (1oz) sieved cocoa for 25g (1oz) of the flour and proceed as above.

115

Preserves and confectionery

Preserves cooked in a microwave oven, especially jams and marmalades, retain their fresh colour. The kitchen, and the cook, remain cooler and there are no sticky saucepans to wash up afterwards. Always use a very large ovenproof bowl or container, and make smaller rather than larger quantities at a time, to prevent boiling over. Test jams and marmalades for setting in the normal way, and leave them to stand before pouring into jars to be sealed and labelled.

Confectionery such as fudge and coconut ice is fairly easy to make in the oven. Again, use a very large ovenproof bowl, and do not leave unattended during the cooking period. When stirring during cooking stir gently, since mixture may rise in the bowl.

Raspberry jam *(makes about 1kg/2lb)*

450g (1lb) raspberries
450g (1lb) preserving or granulated sugar

1 Place raspberries in a large 3 litre (5¼pt) ovenproof bowl and microwave on HIGH for 5 min or until soft.
2 Add the sugar and stir until dissolved.
3 Microwave on HIGH for 15 min or until setting point is reached (105°C/221°F). Stir every 5 min.
4 Leave to stand and cool slightly. Stir.
5 Pour into sterilised jars. Cover, seal and label in the usual way.

Note: *Always use oven gloves or a cloth to handle the bowl when making preserves, since it does get very hot.*

VARIATION
Strawberry Jam: substitute 450g (1lb) strawberries, not over-ripe, for raspberries. Add 1tbsp lemon juice to strawberries at step 1 above. Reduce sugar to 350g (12oz) and proceed as above.

Lemon curd *(makes about 450g/1lb)*

75g (3oz) butter, cut into small pieces
2 lemons, finely grated rind and juice
150g (6oz) caster sugar
3 eggs

1 Place the butter in an ovenproof bowl and microwave on HIGH for 2 min or until melted.
2 Beat together the remaining ingredients in a 1.4 litre (2½pt) ovenproof bowl.
3 Microwave on HIGH for 3 min, stirring every minute.
4 Continue cooking on HIGH for a further 1½ min or until mixture is thick enough to coat the back of a spoon. It is essential to whisk or beat every 30 sec at this stage to prevent curdling.
5 After removing from the oven whisk the mixture till cool, or liquidise in a blender for 30–60 sec.
6 Pour into small sterilised jars. Seal and label in the usual way.

Note: *Lemon curd does not keep very well, so it is best made in small quantities and stored in a refrigerator for up to a month.*

Marmalade *(makes about 2.8kg/5lb)*

2 lemons
2 oranges
2 grapefruit
900ml (1½pt) boiling water
1.8kg (4lb) preserving or granulated sugar.

1 Cut the fruit in half, squeeze out the juice and set aside.
2 Remove pips and pith from the skins and tie in a piece of muslin.
3 Shred the peel finely or coarsely, as preferred.
4 Place the reserved juice and peel in a large ovenproof bowl at least 3 litre (5¼pt) capacity. Add the muslin bag.
5 Add 300ml (½pt) of the water and leave to stand for at least 1 hr. Remove the muslin bag.
6 Stir in the remaining 600ml (1pt) boiling water and cover the bowl with plastic wrap.
7 Microwave on HIGH for 25–30 min or until peel is tender. Time will depend on thickness of peel.
8 Add sugar, and stir until dissolved.
9 Cook, uncovered, on HIGH for a further 30 min or until setting point is reached (105°C/221°F). Stir every 5 min, and check regularly for setting after 25 min.
10 Leave to stand to cool slightly.
11 Stir and pour into sterilised jars. Cover, seal and label in the usual way.

Note: *Always use oven gloves or a cloth to handle the bowl when making preserves, since it does get very hot.*

Rhubarb and ginger jam *(makes about 1.5kg/3lb)*

675g (1½lb) rhubarb, sliced
675g (1½lb) preserving or granulated sugar
2 lemons, juice
15g (½oz) root ginger, bruised and tied in muslin
50g (2oz) preserved ginger

1 Layer the rhubarb with the sugar and lemon juice in a large 3 litre (5¼pt) ovenproof bowl. Cover and leave overnight.

2 Next day add the root ginger and microwave on HIGH for 10 min or until boiling. Stir after 5 min.
3 Continue cooking on HIGH for a further 20 min, stirring after 10 min.
4 Remove the root ginger, add the preserved ginger and microwave on HIGH for a further 5 min or until setting point is reached (105°C/221°F).
5 Leave to stand to cool slightly.
6 Stir and pour into sterilised jars. Seal and label in the usual way.

Note: *Always use oven gloves or a cloth to handle the bowl when making preserves, since it does get very hot.*

Piccalilli *(makes about 1.1kg/2½lb)*

225g (8oz) cauliflower florets
225g (8oz) cucumber, chopped
225g (8oz) peeled marrow, or courgettes, chopped
225g (8oz) very small button or pickling onions, peeled
salt
450ml (¾pt) malt vinegar
1×5ml tsp (1tsp) mustard powder
2×5ml tsp (2tsp) turmeric
½×5ml tsp (½tsp) ground ginger
75g (3oz) caster sugar
1×15ml tbsp (1tbsp) cornflour

1 Layer the vegetables with plenty of salt between each layer. Cover and set aside for 24 hr.
2 Rinse and drain the vegetables thoroughly.
3 Blend 300ml (½pt) of the vinegar with the mustard, turmeric, ginger and sugar in a large 3 litre (5¼pt) ovenproof bowl.
4 Microwave on HIGH for 4 min.
5 Stir in the vegetables, cover and cook on HIGH for about 10 min, depending on how crisp you like the vegetables. Stir after 5 min.
6 Blend the cornflour with the remaining 150ml (¼pt) vinegar.
7 Stir a little of the hot liquid from the vegetables into the cornflour mixture, then stir it all back into the vegetables, mixing well together.

8 Microwave on HIGH for a further 5 min, or until thickened. Stir every minute.
9 Leave to stand for 10 min.
10 Pour into sterilised jars. Seal and label in the usual way.
11 Store for about a month before using to allow flavours to mature.

Note: *Always use oven gloves or a cloth to handle the bowl, since it does get very hot.*

Green tomato chutney *(makes about 1kg/2lb)*

1 medium onion, peeled and finely chopped
675g (1½lb) green tomatoes, chopped
1×225g (8oz) cooking apple, peeled, cored and chopped
100g (4oz) sultanas
150g (6oz) demerara or soft brown sugar
450ml (¾pt) malt vinegar
2×5ml tsp (2tsp) salt
good pinch of cayenne pepper

1 Place the onion with 1tbsp water in an oven-proof bowl.
2 Cover and cook on HIGH for 3 min or until tender. Drain.
3 Place the onion with the remaining ingredients in a large ovenproof bowl, 3 litres (5¼pt) capacity.
4 Cover and microwave on HIGH for 25 min, stirring during this time.
5 Uncover, stir well and continue cooking on HIGH for a further 20–30 min or until thickened to preferred consistency.
6 Leave to stand to cool slightly.
7 Pour into sterilised jars. Cover, seal and label in the usual way.
8 Store for at least one month to allow chutney to mature.

Note: *Always use oven gloves or a cloth to handle the bowl when making chutney, since it does get very hot.*

Coconut ice *(makes about 675g/1½lb)*

450g (1lb) granulated sugar
150ml (¼pt) milk
150g (6oz) desiccated coconut
vanilla essence, optional
cochineal food colouring

1 Place the sugar and milk in a large 3 litre (5¼pt) ovenproof bowl. Stir well.
2 Microwave on HIGH for 4 min, stirring after 2 min.
3 Continue cooking on HIGH for a further 5 min or until mixture reaches 116°C (250°F). Stir every 2 min and check after 4 min. Use oven gloves to handle bowl.
4 Stir in the coconut and essence, if used.
5 Beat the mixture until it thickens, then pour half into a greased tin or dish measuring about 20cm×15cm (8in×6in).
6 Add colouring to remaining mixture and pour quickly over the white mixture.
7 When half set, mark into squares, and cut or break when cold.

Chocolate walnut fudge
(makes about 675g/1½lb)

450g (1lb) icing sugar, sieved
100g (4oz) butter, cut into small pieces
100g (4oz) plain chocolate, broken into small pieces
3×15ml tbsp (3tbsp) milk
50g (2oz) walnut pieces
vanilla essence, optional

1 Place sugar, butter, chocolate and milk in a large 3 litre (5¼pt) ovenproof bowl.
2 Microwave on HIGH for 3 min or until butter and chocolate have melted. Stir after 1½ min.
3 Beat mixture until smooth.
4 Stir in nuts and essence, if used.
5 Pour into a buttered 17.5cm (7in) square tin.
6 Cool, and refrigerate until set.
7 Cut into squares when cold.

Bread-mix loaf (page 107); Fruit scones (page 114); Treacle scones (page 108); Preserves (pages 116–18); Chocolate walnut fudge (above)

Chocolate coconut pyramids

225g (8oz) milk or plain chocolate flavoured
 cake covering
100g (4oz) desiccated coconut

1 Break the cake covering into small pieces into
 an ovenproof bowl.
2 Microwave on HIGH for 2½ min or until
 melted. Stir after 1 and 2 min.
3 Stir in coconut, mixing until thoroughly
 coated in chocolate.
4 Leave to cool slightly.
5 Using two forks, place in small heaps in paper
 sweet cases.
6 Refrigerate until hard.

Treacle toffee *(makes about 550g/1¼lb)*

100g (4oz) butter
225g (8oz) caster or soft brown sugar
225g (8oz) black treacle

1 Place the butter, sugar and treacle in a large 3
 litre (5¼pt) ovenproof bowl.
2 Microwave on HIGH for 1½–2 min or until the
 sugar has dissolved, stirring every 30 sec.
3 Continue cooking on HIGH, without stirring,
 for a further 5 min or until the mixture
 reaches 138°C (280°F).
4 Pour into a well-greased 17.5cm (7in) square
 tin and leave to set.
5 Mark into squares when cool. Cut and wrap
 in waxed paper when cold.
6 Store in an airtight jar.

Vanilla fudge *(makes about 550g/1¼lb)*

450g (1lb) granulated sugar
50g (2oz) butter, cut into small pieces
150ml (¼pt) evaporated milk
150ml (¼pt) milk
½×5ml tsp (½tsp) vanilla essence, or to taste

1 Place the sugar, butter and milks into a large
 3 litre (5¼pt) ovenproof bowl.
2 Microwave on HIGH for 4 min or until boiling. Stir after 2 min.
3 Stir until sugar is dissolved.
4 Microwave on HIGH for a further 15 min or
 until mixture reaches 116°C (240°F). Stir
 every 4 min.
5 Use oven gloves to remove bowl from oven,
 and place on a protected work surface.
6 Stir in vanilla essence, then beat mixture until
 it is thick, creamy and of a 'grainy' consistency.
7 Pour into a well-buttered 15cm (6in) square
 tin.
8 Mark into squares when cool, and cut when
 cold.
9 Store in an airtight container.

Note: *When making fudge or other confectionery in a microwave oven do not leave it unattended. When stirring during cooking stir
gently, since mixture may rise in bowl.*

Chocolate nutty delights *(makes 12)*

50g (2oz) plain chocolate, broken into small
 pieces
12 maraschino cherries
chopped nuts

1 Place the chocolate in a small ovenproof bowl
 and microwave on HIGH for about 45 sec or
 until melted. Stir after 30 sec.
2 Dip the cherries in the melted chocolate and
 then in the chopped nuts and leave until the
 chocolate has set.

VARIATION
Substitute other fruits such as pineapple cubes,
fresh strawberries, melon balls or orange seg-
ments. Marshmallows are also suitable.

. . . In addition

Croûtons (serves 4)

2 large thick slices white or brown bread
40g (1½oz) butter, cut into small pieces

1 Remove the crusts from the bread and cut into 1.25 (½in) cubes.
2 Place the butter in a shallow ovenproof dish and microwave on HIGH for 1 min or until melted.
3 Add the bread cubes, stirring to coat with the butter.
4 Microwave on HIGH for 1½ min. Rearrange or stir after 1 min.
5 Turn the bread cubes over and microwave on HIGH for a further 1½ min or until firm but not crisp. Rearrange or stir after 1 min. The croûtons will crisp during standing time.
6 Drain on absorbent kitchen paper and stand for 2 min.
7 Serve with soup, either separately or sprinkled over.

Note: *It is important to rearrange the croûtons during cooking, to prevent any being overcooked or burned.*

VARIATIONS
Herb croûtons: mix 1tsp fresh or ½tsp dried herbs with the melted butter and bread cubes. Proceed as above.
Garlic croûtons: stir a minced garlic clove, or a little garlic salt, into the melted butter and bread cubes. Proceed as above.
Parmesan croûtons: toss the cooked drained croûtons in 15g (½oz) grated Parmesan cheese.

Bacon rolls

225g (8oz) streaky bacon, de-rinded

1 Remove any pieces of bone from the bacon rashers.
2 Stretch the rashers with the back of a knife, cut each one in half and roll up fairly loosely.
3 Place the rolls with the ends underneath, preferably on a microwave roasting rack in a dish. Alternatively arrange the rolls on a large Pyrex or ovenproof plate without metal trim.
4 Cover with kitchen paper and microwave on HIGH for 3 min.
5 Rearrange the rolls, re-cover and cook on HIGH for a further 4 min or until cooked as preferred.
6 Serve with roast poultry. Cook while poultry is left to stand after cooking.

Dried breadcrumbs

2 large slices brown or white bread, crusts removed

1 Arrange the bread in a single layer on kitchen paper on the floor of the oven.
2 Microwave on HIGH for 2–3 min. Check after every minute. Time taken to dry will depend on freshness of bread. Do not overheat or the bread will burn.
3 When dry, break into pieces and crumb in an electric blender or food processor. Alternatively place the pieces in a polythene bag and crush with a rolling pin.

Toasted coconut

50g (2oz) desiccated coconut – no more

1 Spread the coconut on a flat dish or plate.
2 Microwave on HIGH for 4 min or until golden brown.
3 Stir and check every minute. Do not leave unattended since the coconut will burn easily.

Note: *Coconut will continue to darken after it is removed from the oven.*

Garlic bread

1 crusty French loaf
100–125g (4–5oz) butter
4 cloves garlic, chopped finely or 1½×5ml tsp (1½tsp) garlic powder

1 Cut the bread into 2.5cm (1in) thick slices, cutting to, but not through, the bottom of the loaf.
2 If necessary, soften the butter in the oven by placing it, cut up, in an ovenproof bowl and heating on LOW for about 1 min. Do not allow it to melt.
3 Beat the garlic or garlic powder into the butter and spread between the slices.
4 Place the loaf on kitchen paper on the floor of the oven.
5 Microwave on HIGH for 1 min or until just warm to the touch. Do not overheat.
6 Serve at once.

VARIATION
1 **Herb bread:** omit garlic and add 2tsp dried oregano, 2tsp dried basil and 1tsp celery seed to the softened butter. Proceed as above.
2 **Cheese bread:** omit garlic and add 50g (2oz) grated Parmesan to the softened butter. Proceed as above.

Shrove Tuesday pancakes *(serves 4)*

4 pancakes, cooked conventionally and frozen interleaved with freezer tissue or plastic wrap
caster sugar
lemon wedges

1 Place the frozen layered pancakes on an ovenproof plate without metal trim.
2 Microwave on LOW for 2–2½ min or until warm and pliable. Remove tissue or plastic wrap.
3 Serve sprinkled with caster sugar, accompanied by lemon wedges.

Note:
1 2 frozen pancakes will require about 1½ min on LOW to defrost.
2 If filled pancakes are preferred proceed as above to step 2. Spread with filling of choice, either savoury or sweet, roll up and heat on HIGH as follows:
4 pancakes with savoury filling 2½–3 min
4 pancakes with sweet filling 1½–2 min
2 pancakes with savoury filling 1–1½ min
2 pancakes with sweet filling 45–60 sec.

Toasted flaked almonds

25g (1oz) butter
100g (4oz) blanched flaked almonds

1 Place butter in a shallow ovenproof dish and microwave on HIGH for 45 sec or until melted.
2 Stir in almonds and microwave on HIGH for 5 min or until golden brown. Stir after every minute.
3 Leave to cool on absorbent kitchen paper.

VARIATION
Salted almonds: use 50g (2oz) butter and 225g (8oz) shelled skinned almonds. Place the butter and almonds in a large shallow ovenproof dish and microwave on HIGH for 5 min, stirring after every minute. Turn onto absorbent kitchen paper and toss in salt, preferably sea salt, while hot.

Parsley dumplings (serves 4–6)

50g (2oz) self-raising wholewheat flour
50g (2oz) self-raising white flour
50g (2oz) shredded suet
$\frac{1}{2}$×5ml tsp ($\frac{1}{2}$tsp) salt
1×15ml tbsp (1tbsp) chopped parsley
4×15ml tbsp (4tbsp) cold water, approximately

1 Combine the flours, suet, salt and parsley in a mixing bowl.
2 Add enough water to give a soft but not sticky dough.
3 Divide mixture into 8 to 12 pieces and form each piece into a small ball.
4 Place the dumplings on top of a simmering stew or casserole, preferably in a ring around the outside.
5 Cover the dish with a tight-fitting lid or plastic wrap, allowing room for the dumplings to rise during cooking, and microwave on HIGH for 5 min or until well risen and cooked.

VARIATION
Herb dumplings: substitute 1tsp dried mixed herbs or 2tsp freshly chopped mixed herbs for parsley.

Fruit juice (makes 750ml/1$\frac{1}{4}$pt)

1×178ml (6$\frac{1}{4}$oz) frozen orange or grapefruit concentrate
water

1 Hold the unopened container briefly under warm running water to loosen the frozen block of juice.
2 Open the container and empty the contents into a Pyrex or non-metallic measuring jug.
3 Microwave on HIGH for 1$\frac{1}{2}$ min, breaking up with a fork during this time. Do not leave the fork in the oven.
4 Add water according to manufacturer's instructions.
5 Stir well and leave to stand for a few minutes, if necessary, to completely defrost, before serving.

Basic stock (makes about 900ml/1$\frac{1}{2}$pt)

1 chicken carcass, broken up, plus chicken bones or 450g (1lb) meat or ham bones
1 medium onion, quartered
1 stick of celery, roughly chopped
1 carrot, roughly chopped
bouquet garni
salt and pepper
900ml (1$\frac{1}{2}$pt) hot water

1 Place all ingredients in a large bowl, of at least 2.8 litre (5pt) capacity.
2 Cover and microwave on HIGH, allowing at least 20 min for chicken stock and 40 min for meat stock.
3 Leave to stand, covered, until cool.
4 Strain the stock through a fine sieve.
5 Refrigerate when cold.
6 Remove any fat from the surface before use.

Crumb case for flans, pies, cheesecakes (makes 1×22.5cm/9in case)

100g (4oz) butter or margarine
225g (8oz) digestive biscuits, crushed
40g (1$\frac{1}{2}$oz) demerara sugar, optional

1 Place the butter or margarine in a 22.5cm (9in) ovenproof flan dish or pie plate.
2 Microwave on HIGH for 75 sec or until melted.
3 Stir in the biscuit crumbs and the sugar if used.
4 Press the mixture evenly over the base and sides of the container, using the back of a spoon.
5 Microwave on HIGH for 1$\frac{1}{2}$ min to set the crust.
6 Leave to cool, refrigerate and use as required.

Notes: *For a 17.5cm (7–8in) crumb case, use 75g (3oz) butter or margarine, 150g (6oz) digestive biscuits, crushed, and 25g (1oz) demerara sugar, optional. Proceed as above.*

VARIATION
Use ginger or chocolate wholemeal biscuits instead of digestive biscuits and proceed as above.

Microwave short cuts

Citrus fruits will be easier to squeeze and will give more juice if heated for just 30 sec on HIGH setting.

A fresh peach is more easily skinned if it is first heated for 15–30 sec on HIGH setting.

Dried fruit such as currants, raisins or sultanas which have been stored for some time can easily be plumped. Simply place in an ovenproof bowl and barely cover with water. Cover bowl and microwave on HIGH for about 3 min. Stir and leave to stand, covered, for 5 min.

Dry herbs by heating them on kitchen paper until dry and crumbly. Times vary depending on variety and quantity. Check at 30 sec intervals.

Freshen a stale bread roll by heating for 10 sec. Serve warm.

Ice-cream is easier to scoop if heated for a few seconds.

Brie and Camembert cheese can be ripened using LOW setting allowing about 30 sec for 75g (3oz). Leave to stand for a few minutes before serving.

Melt 100g (4oz) chocolate in an ovenproof bowl in 1½ min. Stir after 1 min.

Food to be cooked on a barbecue can be partly cooked in a microwave oven before placing over the hot coals. This will prevent burning the outside of food to cook the inside, a common fault with barbecues.

Soften refrigerated butter to make it easier to spread. A 250g (8oz) pack, removed from its wrapper and placed on a non-metallic plate, will soften after 30–45 sec on LOW setting. Soften cream cheese in the same way.

Small amounts of jam left in the bottom of jars need not be wasted. Remove metal cap from jar, place jar in oven and heat on HIGH for 10–20 sec, depending on quantity.

Left-over cold coffee is quickly reheated on HIGH. Allow 1½ min per cup.

Packet jellies can be quickly dissolved by placing the cut up cubes in an ovenproof bowl and adding 150ml (¼pt) water. Microwave on HIGH for 1½ min, or until cubes have melted. Make up to required amount with water and ice cubes.

Dissolve gelatine in water in seconds on HIGH. For example 15g (½oz) gelatine in 3tbsp of water only requires 15–30 sec. Stir until completely dissolved.

Index